Giacomo Meyerbeer

The Deliberately Forgotten Composer

DAVID FAIMAN

DISCARD

Copyright © David Faiman
Jerusalem 2020/5780

All rights reserved. No part of this publication may be translated, reproduced, stored in a retrieval system or transmitted, in any form or by any means, electronic, mechanical, photocopying, recording or otherwise, without express written permission from the publishers.

Grateful acknowledgment is extended to Robert Letellier for permission to quote from Robert Ignatius Letellier, trans. and ed., *The Diaries of Giacomo Meyerbeer*, 4 vols. (Cranbury, NJ: Associated University Presses, 1999) as well as from *Giacomo Meyerbeer: A Reader* (Newcastle, UK: Cambridge Scholars Publishing, 2007) and from Richard Arsenty and Robert Ignatius Letellier, *Giacomo Meyerbeer: The Complete Libretti in Five Volumes* (Newcastle, UK: Cambridge Scholars Publishing, 2004); to Mark Violette for permission to quote from his translation of *Giacomo Meyerbeer: Ein Leben in Briefen* by Heinz and Gudrun Becker (Portland, OR: Amadeus Press, 1989); to Rowman and Littlefield for permission to quote from Patrick Barbier, *Opera in Paris, 1800–1850: A Lively History*, trans. Robert Luoma (Portland, OR: Amadeus Press, 1995); to Suhrkamp Verlag for permission to quote from Hal Draper, *The Complete Poems of Heinrich Heine. A Modern English Version* (Boston: Suhrkamp/Insel Publishers, 1982); to Kensington Books for permission to quote from the translations of Heine's poems by Frederic Ewen, trans. and ed., *The Poetry and Prose of Heinrich Heine* (New York: Citadel Press, 1959); to Royal Collection Trust / © Her Majesty Queen Elizabeth II 2020 for permission to reproduce Coronation scene from Meyerbeer's *Le Prophète* by Edward Henry Corbould; to the Victoria and Albert Museum, London, for permission to reproduce *The Ballet Scene from Meyerbeer's Opera Robert le Diable* by Edgar Degas; to Stadtmuseum Berlin / Hans-und-Luise-Richter-Stiftung for permission to reproduce the portrait of Jacob Herz Beer, pastel by Johann Heinrich Schröder, 1797, photographed by Hans-Joachim Bartsch, Berlin; to Marco Pellegrini for permission to quote from his translation of Giuseppe Mazzini's letter to Emilie Venturi, May 21, 1867; to University of California Press for permission to quote from David Cairns, *Berlioz*, vol. 2, *Servitude and Greatness* (Berkeley: University of California Press, 2000), copyright 2000 by the Regents of the University of California; all attempts at tracing the copyright holder of *The Memoirs of Hector Berlioz*, translated, edited, and introduced by David Cairns (London: Victor Gollancz, 1969) were unsuccessful; likewise for Mordechai Golinkin, *Mi-Heichalei Yefet l'Ohalei Shem* (Tel Aviv: privately published, 1957).

Cover Design: Leah Ben Avraham/Noonim Graphics
Cover Illustration: Avi Katz
Typesetting: Raphaël Freeman MISTD, Renana Typesetting
Rear cover photo: selfie of the author

ISBN: 978-965-7023-15-0

1 3 5 7 9 8 6 4 2

Gefen Publishing House Ltd.
6 Hatzvi Street
Jerusalem 9438614, Israel
972-2-538-0247

Gefen Books
c/o 3PL Center, 3003 Woodbridge Ave.
Edison, NJ 08837
516-593-1234

orders@gefenpublishing.com
www.gefenpublishing.com

Printed in Israel

Library of Congress Control Number: 2020901138

Contents

Preface	vii
Acknowledgments	xi
Introduction	1
Chapter 1: Childhood	11
Chapter 2: Serious Studies	20
Chapter 3: The Land Where Lemons Blossom	29
Chapter 4: Paris at Last!	43
Chapter 5: Superstar Status	58
Chapter 6: A Brief Interlude in Berlin	70
Chapter 7: Two Comic Operas	81
Chapter 8: An Unexpected End	89
Chapter 9: Meyerbeer's Music	98
Chapter 10: Meyerbeer the Man	119
Chapter 11: The Falling Star	137
Chapter 12: Meyerbeer and Anti-Semitism	148
Chapter 13: The Case of Richard Wagner	166
Chapter 14: Meyerbeer in Israel	183
Chapter 15: Finale	202
Appendix 1: Early Meyerbeer Recordings	216
Appendix 2: Palestine Opera Productions	219
An Annotated Bibliography	221
Index	227

Preface

This book is the true story of a composer who was born in 1791, the year that Wolfgang Amadeus Mozart died, and who departed this world in 1864, the year in which Richard Strauss was born. The name by which he was known to the world was Giacomo Meyerbeer. During his first fifty years he grew to become one of the most famous composers of opera who had ever lived. His operas were performed in all self-respecting opera houses the world over. When he died, he received a state funeral in his homeland, and his loss was mourned by the music-loving public everywhere. Royalty and some of the most prominent composers of the time were distraught at the loss to music. By the time gramophone records came into existence at around the start of the twentieth century – with their three- to four-minute-per-side capacity – many hundreds of vocal recordings of extracts from his operas had been made, by all the famous singers of the time: the soprano Lilli Lehmann, the contralto Sigrid Onegin, the tenor Enrico Caruso, and the bass Feodor Chaliapin, to name but four. These and other stars from that so-called "golden age" of voice, for whom Meyerbeer was standard repertoire, have left us copious proof of his position among composers of opera. Nevertheless, today, many lovers of opera have never even heard the name Meyerbeer, and among those who have, few will be acquainted with his music. Is it not strange that within a period of about half a century, one of the world's most famous composers came to be so neglected?

To see how improbable such a situation is, suppose that some authoritative music critic were to claim that Beethoven's music is bombastic rubbish, but so cleverly constructed as to have hoodwinked the entire music-loving world into thinking that it was true art. If that critic were to have a sufficiently large reputation and ego, he might even make such a claim without feeling the need to explain on musical grounds why Beethoven's music is rubbish. Indeed, if that critic's reputation were to be truly enormous, his fellow music critics might even close their eyes to the fact that he had not attempted to justify his claim on musical grounds. They might even feel nervous about voicing out loud any doubts about such an authoritative claim. But what about the music-loving public: Are we so easily taken in? For us that authoritative critic might appeal to the pity we all naturally feel for deaf people, and our mistaken awe that a deaf man like Beethoven could have produced such beautiful music. Such a situation could not, of course, happen, could it?

In fact it did. Not to Ludwig van Beethoven, but to the composer whose childhood name was Meyer Beer. And the authoritative critic who destroyed Beer's reputation, caused his music to be removed from our opera houses and concert halls, and who all but eliminated his name from the history of music was a man by the name of Richard Wagner.

Unlike Beethoven, Meyerbeer was not deaf, but he had an even worse impediment as far as Wagner was concerned: he was a Jew. Moreover, with the latent anti-Semitism of nineteenth-century European audiences, it did not take too long for Wagner and his followers to discredit Meyerbeer and his operas to such an extent that his very name became associated with everything that is distasteful in music. His operas gradually disappeared from sight, being replaced by the initially less "popular" but supposedly infinitely "deeper" works of Wagner.

Until very recently, Meyerbeer's operas were rarely performed. And yet, on those fortunately increasing occasions when they are performed, as the author of this book can attest from several personal experiences, they are usually met with enormous enthusiasm by their audiences. On the other hand, the newspaper reports of these events are often less enthusiastic, critics – previously unacquainted with his works – having looked up "Meyerbeer" in an encyclopedia and read that his music is worthless. To this day, in Israel, a country that one might think would have spearheaded the Meyerbeer revival, the Israel Opera has never performed any of his operas, and it is only within the past few years that they are beginning to return to European stages – principally in Germany and France – after an absence of approximately a century.

This book will tell the story of Meyerbeer's life and his reluctant rise to superstar status; introduce, in a convenient format, his music and some recommended recordings; and will delve into the cause of the disappearance of the music and the very name of its composer, a uniquely catastrophic fall from fame. It is not a scholarly book in that published English translations have been quoted rather than the original sources, which are usually in French, German, or Italian.

The book was originally intended principally for Israeli readers because no book on Meyerbeer has yet been written in Hebrew, and no Meyerbeer opera has been performed in Israel since 1927 when Mordechai Golinkin and his short-lived Palestine Opera staged the last of eleven performances of *Les Huguenots* – in Hebrew translation! However, for readers of this book's English version, it will hopefully serve as an introduction to the more in-depth Meyerbeer studies that have begun to appear in that language in recent years, which are referenced in the footnotes. Nevertheless, whichever version of this book is encountered, it is hoped that it will encourage readers to explore the largely forgotten riches of Meyerbeer's music.

Acknowledgments

This book would not have been possible without the friendship and encouragement of Dr. Robert Letellier, whose four-volume, richly annotated English translation of Meyerbeer's diaries has been copiously quoted, and which must surely form a foundation for any serious study of the composer. The author has also benefitted significantly from conversations and or written exchanges with musicologists Marco Beghelli, Leon Botstein, Mark Everist, and Jennifer Jackson. Their writings on Meyerbeer, together with those of Robert Letellier (in addition to his translations of the diaries), must be reckoned among the most important contributions to contemporary Meyerbeer scholarship. The author also acknowledges having derived much insight from the writings of Joachim Köhler and Gottfried Wagner. It was the latter who first drew his attention to the special role that his great-grandfather Richard had played in the Meyerbeer story.

Among advocates of the Meyerbeer cause, whose friendship the author cherishes, Volker Tosta stands out for his resurrection of *Alimelek*. A special place must also be reserved for Stephen Agus, founder of the Meyerbeer Fan Club, who has infused the club's rich website with great wisdom and has promoted several Meyerbeer concerts, among which were the first Tel Aviv production of *Gli Amore di Teolinda* and the New York premiere of Charles-Valentin

Alkan's piano reduction of the original (and later abandoned) overture to *Le Prophète*.

Several musicians have enriched the author's understanding of Meyerbeer's music. Particularly: choirmaster Avner Itai, sopranos Andrea Chudak and Sivan Rotem, conductors Dario Salvi and Mark Wolloch, composer Michael Wolpe, and pianist Jonathan Zak. In this regard, special appreciation is due to the author's nephew, the composer Jonathan Faiman, who has devoted significant quantities of his time and knowledge to creating modern performing scores from difficult-to-read photocopies of Meyerbeer manuscripts and from ancient printed editions with archaic musical notation.

The author also wishes to express special appreciation to the following friends who read various earlier versions of this book and who gently pointed out an embarrassingly large number of errors: Shulamit Amir-Zarmi, Nicky Avery, Louis Beck, Shoshana Dann, Ofra Faiman, Jennifer Kaheil, Robert Letellier, Donald M. Reid, Jeff Stephens, Rosalind Weinberg, and Walter Wiertz. Publisher Ilan Greenfield at Gefen Publishing House believed in the importance of this book from the start, and Project Manager Daphne Abrahams ably shepherded the book through the stages of production, which included the elegant typesetting and layout of Raphaël Freeman. Apropos of production, the author is particularly beholden to Wikipedia for their Wikimedia Commons collection of public domain photographs. Finally, no words of praise can be strong enough for Kezia Raffel Pride, Senior Editor at Gefen, who left no stone unturned in researching each detail in the submitted manuscript and whose numerous astute comments led to a greatly improved book. Some errors must surely remain, for which only the author should be held responsible.

The author will forever be indebted to all of the wonderful people – too numerous to list or even to know by name – who were involved in bringing about those Meyerbeer opera performances that he and his wife have thus far been privileged to behold: *Margherita d'Anjou*

(London, 2002, and Leipzig, 2005); *Dinorah* (Compiegne, 2004); *Les Huguenots* (Metz, 2004, and Annandale-on-Hudson, 2009); *L'Africaine* (Strasbourg, 2004; Gelsenkirchen, 2008; and Berlin, 2016); *Semiramide* (Bad Wildbad, 2005); *Le Prophète* (Amsterdam, 2008; Braunschweig, 2014; and Karlsruhe, 2016); *Alimelek* (Bad Urach, 2010); *Robert le Diable* (Erfurt, 2012, and London, 2012).

Finally, this book could not have been written without the loving encouragement and support of the author's dear wife Ofra, who accompanied him to all these Meyerbeer performances, and whose deeply artistic insight has contributed in no small measure to his understanding and enjoyment of these works.

Introduction

Many lovers of what is commonly referred to as "classical music" will not be familiar with the music of Giacomo Meyerbeer, even though when he died in 1864 the obituary that appeared in the *Illustrated London News* began with the words "The death of this illustrious composer has made a greater blank in the musical world than has been made since the death of Mendelssohn, nearly twenty years ago."

Toward the end of the piece its writer surmised, "His history must be the history of his art-progress, and the successive births of those great works which will give lasting celebrity to his name...."

"Great works"? What are they? "Lasting celebrity"? Then how has it come about that so few people have even heard the name Meyerbeer?

If this were a book on, say, Antonio Vivaldi, it would doubtless make fascinating reading. A musical genius born in 1678, whose compositions and even name, owing to the combined quirks of history and geography, came to be totally forgotten: yes, totally. That was, until the twentieth century revealed *Le quattro stagioni* (the Four Seasons) and the plethora of glorious musical compositions that gradually followed that remarkable discovery. Today most people would find it hard to believe that for over a century the name and music of Vivaldi were totally unknown to music lovers.

The story of Meyerbeer's music and name is somewhat similar to that of Vivaldi's. However, there are two enormous differences between the two cases. First, during his lifetime, Vivaldi's compositions were hardly known beyond the walls of the school for foundlings in Venice where he taught music. In contrast, Meyerbeer, at his death in 1864, was arguably the most celebrated opera composer in the entire world. His creations were staple fare in all serious opera houses across the globe, and his virtuoso roles were performed by all the greatest singers. Stars such as Jennie Lind (the "Swedish Nightingale"), Nellie Melba (of Peach Melba fame), and the de Reszke brothers (immortalized by Sherlock Holmes) earned astronomical salaries for their Meyerbeer roles. As a typical example: in June 1905, Enrico Caruso was invited to perform in act 4 of Meyerbeer's most famous opera, *Les Huguenots*, at a special command performance at Buckingham Palace, in honor of a visit to King Edward VII by the king of Spain.[1] Like Melba and Caruso, all the famous opera singers who recorded during the early years of sound recordings have left us adequate proof of their regard for Meyerbeer's mastery of his art. Indeed, cylinders and shellac discs are known for no fewer than a thousand singers from that era who recorded more than 150 Meyerbeer arias.[2]

Moreover, Meyerbeer's name was not confined to the opera house, for his celebrity reached far beyond. Mechanical music boxes in the era prior to sound recording could bring his melodies into the homes of those who did not play an instrument. And whether music lovers did or did not play an instrument, a statuette of the composer frequently adorned the mantelpiece.

---

1. Francis Robinson, *Caruso: His Life in Pictures* (New York: Studio Publications, 1957), 72.
2. Richard Arsenty and Robert Ignatius Letellier, *Giacomo Meyerbeer: A Discography of Vintage Recordings, 1889–1955* (Newcastle upon Tyne, UK: Cambridge Scholars Publishing, 2013).

INTRODUCTION

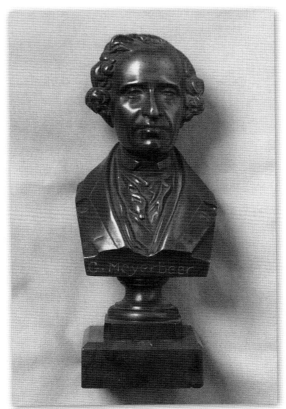

A nineteenth-century statuette of Meyerbeer (David Faiman collection)

Picture postcards portrayed his visage, and a variety of children's trading cards (e.g., those issued by cigarette, chocolate, and meat-extract manufacturers) displayed scenes from his operas.

Hotels and streets were named after him in many cities of the world.

In fact, all manner of Meyerbeer memorabilia flooded the market in a comparable manner to which film stars, pop singers, and sports heroes came to be celebrated in a later era. Perhaps the most remarkable example was "the apotheosis of Meyerbeer" depicting the demi-god surrounded by the operatic characters he had brought to life.

Some picture postcards depicting Meyerbeer (David Faiman collection)

Picture postcard of the Hotel Meyerbeer at Rond-Point in Paris, postmarked April 23, 1914 (David Faiman collection)

The apotheosis of Meyerbeer postcard by Bulla Frères, c. 1865 (Wikimedia Commons)

When he died in Paris, Meyerbeer's funeral cortege was, in pomp and circumstance, like none that had previously been conferred upon any famous person other than royalty. It included a special train that was sent from Prussia to carry his remains back to Berlin for state burial.

So, given that Giacomo Meyerbeer was *so* famous, up to about the start of the First World War, how did it come about that he was so quickly forgotten – to such an extent that this book needs to be written? The answer to that question is the second great difference between Vivaldi's neglect and Meyerbeer's: Vivaldi was accidentally forgotten, but Meyerbeer's memory was deliberately erased!

In 1869, Richard Wagner, by then a well-known composer, wrote:

> A far-famed Jewish tone-setter of our day has addressed himself and products to a section of our public whose total confusion of musical taste was less to be first caused by him, than worked out

to his profit.... There is no object in more closely designating the artistic means he has expended on the reaching of this life's-aim: enough that, as we may see by the result, he knew completely how to dupe.... In fact, this composer pushes his deception so far, that he ends by deceiving himself, and perchance as purposely as he deceives his bored admirers. We believe, indeed, that he honestly would like to turn out artworks, and yet is well aware he cannot: to extricate himself from this painful conflict between Will and Can, he writes operas for Paris, and sends them touring round the world – the surest means, to-day, of earning oneself an art renown albeit not an artist. Under the burden of this self-deception, which may not be so toilless as one might think, he, too, appears to us wellnigh in a tragic light: yet the purely personal element of wounded vanity turns the thing into a tragi-comedy, just as in general the un-inspiring, the truly laughable, is the characteristic mark whereby this famed composer shews his Jewhood in his music.[3]

That "far-famed Jewish tone-setter," whom Wagner, craftily, did not even deign to mention by name, was, as all of his readers at that time would have known, Giacomo Meyerbeer, who had died five years earlier.

At the time of his death, Meyerbeer was arguably the most famous opera composer who had ever lived, and certainly one of the most famous composers of his time. However, as must be clear from even the most cursory reading of the above words, Wagner was employing every dirty trick in the book in order to discourage anyone from imagining that what this "renowned Jewish composer" had produced bore any resemblance to true art.

Wagner, of course, had an enormous influence on artistic taste,

---

3. Richard Wagner, *Das Judenthum in der Musik*, trans. William Ashton Ellis, in *The Theatre: Richard Wagner's Prose Works*, vol. 3 (1894), 79–100.

Giacomo Meyerbeer, engraving from a photograph by Pierre Petit, 1865 (Wikimedia Commons)

matched in enormity only by his own ego. So enormous indeed was his influence that not only were many Jews able to shut their eyes to his blatant anti-Semitism, but several of them even took the closing scurrilous message of his *Das Judenthum in der Musik* (Jewishness in

Music) – the pamphlet from which the above quotation was taken – sufficiently seriously as actually to commit suicide: the only way of removing that Jewish stain with which, according to their master, they had been born. But even among those Jewish Wagnerites who chose life, the anti-Meyerbeer poison penetrated deeply.

This little book presents only the briefest outline of Meyerbeer's life and an introduction to his music. It is intentionally small in order to enable the reader to get through it in a day or two. The story is so unprecedented that some might regard the claim – that jealousy and anti-Semitism were the main causes for the disappearance of Meyerbeer's music – as being so unlikely as to dismiss it as a "conspiracy theory." So the author hastens to add that these conclusions have already been penned to a greater or lesser extent by all late twentieth-century musicologists who are specialists on the history of opera,[4] and by many who were brave enough to voice them during the early years of that century.[5]

Unfortunately, at the time of this writing, there is evidently a great distance between musicologist and opera house manager, which is causing the return of Meyerbeer's operas to the mainstream repertoire to be slow. A further complication is that it is a common

---

4. Robert Ignatius Letellier, *Meyerbeer Studies: A Series of Lectures, Essays, and Articles on the Life and Work of Giacomo Meyerbeer* (Madison, WI: Fairleigh Dickinson University Press, 2005); Mark Everist, *Giacomo Meyerbeer and Music Drama in Nineteenth-Century Paris* (Aldershot, UK: Ashgate Variorum, 2005); Jennifer Jackson, *Giacomo Meyerbeer: Reputation without Cause? A Composer and His Critics* (Newcastle upon Tyne, UK: Cambridge Scholars Publishing, 2011).

5. Herman Klein, in William R. Moran, ed., *Herman Klein and the Gramophone* (Portland, OR: Amadeus Press, 1990), specifically, the articles on pages 114–21, which date from 1925; Cecil Gray, *The History of Music*, 2nd ed. (London: Kegan Paul, Trench, Trubner, 1931), 202–5; Bernard van Dieren, *Down among the Dead Men and Other Essays* (1935; repr., Freeport, NY: Books for Libraries Press, 1967), 142–74.

human weakness that we tend to form our first opinions about anything new from less than firm evidence. Then, once having formed such opinions, it is very difficult for us to accept any facts indicating that our initial opinion may have been totally in error. Thus, the present readers of this book, who may have read something about Meyerbeer, are quite likely to have been preconditioned by the heavily jaundiced – and, as we shall see, totally unfounded – slanders upon the composer's character and music, which started to flood the popular literature – even while his body was still warm. Those readers will be justifiably skeptical about the claim that Meyerbeer's music should be regarded as more than a mere curiosity. Hopefully, the musical examples given here will convince them to reassess their received opinions. On the other hand, readers who have never heard of Meyerbeer will be able to use this brief outline as a first introduction to the life and music of a remarkable composer. They will then, if desire so prompts them, be able to open one of the more detailed contemporary studies that might otherwise have escaped their attention.

Finally, let me switch to the first person, in order to address a personal note to any readers in the future who may happen to come across this little book: I would like to think that just as many of my generation find it hard to believe that Vivaldi's music could ever have been anything but popular, so too will you find it hard to believe that once upon a time Meyerbeer's operas totally disappeared for a century or so. For you then, my book may constitute something of a curiosity. However, let it be a reminder that jealousy and hatred of "the other" can be as deadly in the arts as in the political arena. In his funeral oration of Meyerbeer, Émile Olivier, leader of the French socialists, said:

> May the name of Meyerbeer, the memory of the grief which we share with the people beyond the Rhine, be another pledge of unison between the two sisterly nations, whom nothing should

separate, and let there be a strong and permanent cord between the fatherland of Mozart and Beethoven and the country of Hérold, Halévy and Auber.[6]

As you in your generation along with I and my generation know full well, it would take many years before Olivier's prayer would be fulfilled. However, beautiful music can indeed be a great unifying factor among nations if we embrace that beauty without attaching to it all manner of irrelevant baggage.

---

6. Heinz Becker, "Giacomo Meyerbeer on the Occasion of the Centenary of His Death" in *The Leo Baeck Institute Year Book* 9, no. 1 (January 1964): 178–201, reproduced in Robert Ignatius Letellier, *Giacomo Meyerbeer: A Reader* (Newcastle-upon-Tyne: Cambridge Scholars Publishing, 2007), 389.

Chapter 1
Childhood

It was September 5, 1791. Malka Beer (née Wulff)[1] was on her way east, from the Berlin home where she and her husband, Juda Herz Beer,[2] lived, to the Beer ancestral home in Frankfurt on the river Oder. Malka was at an advanced stage of pregnancy, and she wanted her mother-in-law to attend the birth of her first child. It was not clear whether her husband would be able to join her there owing to business pressures.

However, since such matters were really women's business, it was probably best that Juda should delay his arrival for a day or two, in order for him to be able to see Malka and the baby at their best. Juda and Malka were Jews. By 1791, travel for people of their religion was reasonably safe. This was because three years earlier, Frederick William II, king of Prussia, had brought into law an edict that placed

---

1. Malka Beer (1767–1854) was born Malka Wulff. She started to use the less Semitic-sounding name Amalia after 1812, when Prussian Jews were granted citizenship.
2. Juda Herz (sometimes spelled Hertz) Beer (1769–1825) was a successful sugar merchant. He adopted the name Jacob in preference to Juda from 1812 onwards. He was the son of Naphtali Herz Beer (1736–1808) of Frankfurt on the river Oder and his wife, Jente Enoch Levin (d. 1808).

Malka (later Amalia) Beer, (left), oil by J.K.H. Kretchmar (Wikimedia Commons); Juda (later Jacob) Herz Beer,(right), pastel by Johann Heinrich Schröder, 1797, photographed by Hans-Joachim Bartsch, Berlin (courtesy of and copyright © Stadtmuseum Berlin / Hans-und-Luise-Richter-Stiftung)

all religious affairs under strict control of his Protestant state. Among other things, it granted state protection to the various religious minorities in Prussia. This may sound strange to modern ears, but prior to that edict, Jews who fell prey to highwaymen did not have equal legal status before the law to that enjoyed by citizens: in court cases, they had to depend upon the mercy of the presiding judge.

In fact, in the years before 1812, in spite of the fact that many Jewish families, such as the Wulffs of Berlin and the Beers of Frankfurt, could trace their ancestry back several generations in Prussia, and some had even managed to achieve prominence in business and cultural affairs, Jews had not yet been granted Prussian citizenship. Moreover, there were still harsh laws in force that discriminated against Jewish people in many areas of everyday life. For example, it was not too long in the past that they had not been allowed to marry off more than one child, and for that marriage they were forced to purchase porcelain from the royal potteries. Particularly odious to their dietary tradition had been the requirement for Jews to purchase the wild boar that were shot at royal hunts. Even now, in the 1790s, Jews were not allowed to serve in the Prussian army, and several other prejudicial laws were still in force. For example, Juda had only received the right to reside in Berlin two years before his marriage to Malka. Naturally, the wealthy could manage to minimize the inconvenience of some of these laws, but for the poorer Jews, life was even worse than for poor Christians.

But back to Malka in that carriage to Frankfurt in 1791: things did not turn out precisely as she had planned. At Tasdorf, a few kilometers outside Berlin, the coach suddenly jolted, and she went into labor. It was accordingly there that the birth of her firstborn, Liebmann Meyer, was recorded: not in Frankfurt as she had expected, and not even in the Prussian state capital where the child was to grow up.[3]

Malka named her firstborn in honor of her own father, Liepmann Meyer Wulff,[4] an enormously wealthy businessman who had been blessed with four daughters but no son. It naturally flattered the old man to have a grandson who bore his name, and a special

---

3. The Hebrew date was 6 Elul 5551. In later years, Meyer Beer celebrated his birthdays according to the Hebrew date. The unusual circumstance of Meyer's birth is related in W. Michael Blumenthal, *The Invisible Wall* (Washington, DC: Counterpoint, 1998), 141.
4. The difference in spelling between the grandfather's and grandson's names is apparently a consequence of nonstandardized orthography in German proper names. Liepmann Meyer Wulff (1745–1812) was born in Berlin. He amassed successive fortunes from supplying grain to the Prussian army and from concessions for the Berlin-Potsdam postal route and the Prussian state lottery. His wife was Ester Bamberger (1740–1822), and their four daughters were Malka (1767–1854), Hanka (1770–1847), Sara (1774–1832), and Jette (1779–1852).

relationship was to grow up between him and little Meyer. Malka and Juda went on to have three further children: Heinrich,[5] Wilhelm,[6] and Michael.[7] Of the three, Wilhelm would grow up to become a prominent astronomer, and Michael, though he was not to live many years, would nevertheless become a successful playwright. However, it was for Liebmann Meyer, or "Meyer," as everyone called him, that grandfather Liepmann Meyer manifested special affection.

Like his father-in-law, Juda (or Jacob, the name he adopted after 1812 when Prussian Jews were finally granted citizenship) was also extremely successful in business, and the splendid Berlin home that he and Malka (or Amalia, the official name that she later took) maintained at 72 Spandauer Strasse was a regular gathering ground for the intellectuals and aristocracy of Prussia.

Of relevance to Meyer's intellectual development was the fact that his father devoted a considerable part of his efforts to improving the social standing of his less fortunate coreligionists, with special emphasis on cultural activities. He was one of the founders of a movement to reform the practice of Judaism, in order to try to render its perception less alien to Christians. This included the

---

5. Heinrich Beer (1794–1842) had no lasting fame. However, he married Rebecca Meyer (1793–1850), a first cousin of the composer Felix Mendelssohn (1809–1847), and therefore was instrumental in linking these two Prussian musical families.

6. Wilhelm Beer (1797–1850) became a noted astronomer, who, together with Johann Heinrich Mädler (1794–1874), published the first accurate map of the moon and the first globe of the planet Mars. Both the moon and Mars have craters that have been named after each of these astronomers.

7. Michael Beer (1800–1833) was a noted poet and playwright, whose poetry was much admired by King Ludwig I of Bavaria (the author wishes to thank Elaine Thornton for sharing this information about Ludwig I with him). Meyerbeer created song settings with piano accompaniment (1830) to three of his poems, "Scirocco," "Menschenfeindlich," and "Mina," and later composed incidental music for his play *Struensee* (1846).

use of the German vernacular rather than the traditional Hebrew in religious services, and the introduction of an organ – musical instruments having been banned as an accompaniment to prayer since the destruction of the Jerusalem Temple by the Romans under Titus in 70 CE. Jacob Herz Beer also had a private synagogue in his own home at a time when Jews were not allowed to construct public places of worship.

Amalia, for her part, ran a "salon," which was always well attended by artists, writers, musicians, and others among Berlin's social elite. Like her husband's, Amalia's charitable deeds were outstanding. They went beyond trying to improve the lives of poor Jews. To such an extent was her benevolence, indeed, that in 1816, King Frederick William III would award her the Luisen Orden,[8] a medal in recognition of her charitable activities during Prussia's wars of independence from France (1803–1815). But that was to be far in the future – four years after that king would finally grant Prussian Jews citizenship of the country they had considered home for generations.

But back in the 1790s, little Meyer was growing up and had to be educated in a manner appropriate to a child of his parents' standing in society. Jacob and Amalia engaged the best teachers they could find to develop their son's talents. From an early age Meyer had exhibited unusual musical abilities: it is said that he could recall long and complicated pieces and even compose some of his own. Therefore, a prominent pianist, Ignace Lauska (1769–1825), was engaged as his music tutor. Meyer's pianistic abilities subsequently made rapid progress and, on October 14, 1800, at the tender age of

---

8. It is noteworthy that, out of consideration for her religion, the particular medal that was cast for Amalia Beer did not include the conventional cross that was associated with that order. (Mentioned, together with photographs, in *Juden, Bürger, Berliner: Das Gedächtnis der Familie Beer-Meyerbeer-Richter*, ed. Sven Kuhrau and Kurt Winkler with the assistance of Alice Uebe [Berlin: Henschel, 2004]).

The controversial oil painting of Liebmann Bär by Friedrich Georg Weitsch, 1802 (Wikimedia Commons)

nine, he was able to give his first public concert, which included a concerto by Mozart (who had died a few months after Meyer was born). Moreover, thanks to his mother's influence, a large part of Berlin's musical establishment came to hear him. The critic in the *Allgemeine Musikalische Zeitung* waxed enthusiastic about the remarkable talent of "Liebmann Bär, the new little Jewish virtuoso." Meyer concertized again in 1803 and 1804 with growing success. The composer Muzio Clementi (1752–1832) heard him and is said to have pronounced him a genius, "possibly even a second Mozart."

Following upon Meyer's concert successes, his parents engaged Friedrich Georg Weitsch (1758–1828), a fashionable portrait artist, to paint the young prodigy, and Amalia was able to use her enormous influence to have the painting hung at the Prussian Academy of Arts. However, it hung there for only two weeks. The reason was that, prodigy or not, "No Jew should be allowed to defile the academy's hallowed halls."[9] This was the considered opinion of Prussian Councilor Karl Friedrich Wilhelm Grattenauer (1773–1838), leader of a prominent anti-Semitic movement.

This was the first time that young Meyer discovered for himself that merely being a Jew in Prussia was enough for him to be regarded as an outsider irrespective of his talent – and he was not yet a teenager. However, this early slight, together, possibly, with further explanations and encouragement from his parents, may well have instilled in this musical genius a fierce determination to make a name for himself through success in music.

In 1807, for his Hebrew studies, Meyer's parents engaged Aaron Wolfssohn (c. 1755–1835), one of the leading writers in the so-called Haskalah (Enlightenment) period in Hebrew literature, who had translated and made a commentary on the Hebrew Bible. Wolfssohn was also a playwright and, for the rest of his life, was to become a close friend and confidant of Meyer.

Meyer's home tuition proceeded quickly and smoothly. He took a lively interest in all subjects: literature, history, languages, the arts, etc. This was not surprising, given his natural brilliance and the

---

9. Blumenthal, *The Invisible Wall*, 143.

Famous pedagogue Georg Joseph Vogler (1749–1814), Meyerbeer's teacher in Darmstadt, painted by Franz Durmer, 1790 (Wikimedia Commons)

galaxy of stellar characters who attended his mother's salons. The latter included, for example, the explorer Alexander von Humboldt (1769–1859), who was to become a lifelong friend and supporter, and Friedrich Wilhelm, later to become King Frederick William IV (1840–1861).

Above all, Meyer's musical abilities surged forward. For example, by the age of fifteen, he had already composed a cantata for four voices and orchestra, in honor of Grandfather Liepmann's birthday.[10]

---

10. Sketches for this work, dated 1806, along with other childhood fragments, are to be found in the Meyerbeer *Nachlass* (archive of personal

A few years later, his new teacher, Bernhard Anselm Weber (1764–1821), who had replaced Lauska after the latter had taught the boy all that he could, was so charmed by a fugue Meyer had composed that he proudly sent it to his own former teacher, the venerable Georg Joseph Vogler (1749–1814) in Darmstadt.

Several weeks went by without any response from the learned abbot. Finally, a thick envelope was delivered to the Beer house. It contained a handwritten treatise that Vogler had penned on the art of writing fugues; a heavily marked up "Scholar's fugue," as the master called young Meyer's attempt; and a much lengthier "Master's fugue," which Vogler had constructed on the young man's original theme. Most important, the package was followed up by an invitation for Meyer to attend the famous pedagogue's private school in Darmstadt. However, before setting out, young Meyer had one more commitment in Berlin: his first ballet, *Der Fischer und das Milchmädchen* (The Fisherman and the Milkmaid), produced in March 1810 at the Court Opera.[11]

---

papers), housed in the Staatsbibliothek zu Berlin. The author is indebted to Dr. Roland Schmidt-Hensel for allowing him to study them.

11. See Robert Ignatius Letellier, trans. and ed., *The Diaries of Giacomo Meyerbeer*, vol. 1, *1791–1839* (Cranbury, NJ: Associated University Presses, 1999), 255.

Chapter 2

Serious Studies

On April 15, 1810, Meyer Beer arrived in the city of Darmstadt in order to study music composition under Vogler. Although he was already nineteen years old, his parents sent his tutor, Wolfssohn, and his younger brother, Heinrich, to accompany him on the nearly six-hundred-kilometer journey from Berlin.

Vogler is remembered these days mainly as a pedagogue. However, he was a composer in his own right, one of his requiems having been compared, albeit by himself, not unfavorably with that of Mozart. In addition, he was a renowned organ virtuoso and musical inventor, who created a number of original types of organ.

Mornings at Darmstadt are said to have started with exercises, followed by an oral lesson given by Vogler on a theoretical topic such as harmony, counterpoint, etc.[1] The students were then required to write an original composition on a theme provided by their teacher: typically a psalm, a motet, a dramatic scene, etc. Each of these compositions was then performed in the evening, followed by critical

---

1. This description of the daily studies at Vogler's school is based on the encyclopedia article "Meyerbeer" by Arthur Pougin, in *Famous Composers and Their Music: Extra Illustrated Edition of 1901*, eds. Theodore Thomas, John Knowles Paine, and Karl Klauser (Boston: J.B. Millet, 1901), 473–85.

analysis both by the master and their fellow students. On Sundays, the students were taken to a cathedral where there were two organs. Vogler improvised a theme on one, whereupon the students took it in turns to develop this theme on the other organ. Vogler, being the celebrated organ virtuoso that he was, was particularly impressed with Beer's rapidly acquired organ technique – not surprising since the latter was already a more than proficient pianist – and hoped that he would switch his specialty to the organ. However, Meyer Beer was already exhibiting precocity at composition. Indeed, only six weeks after his first arrival in Darmstadt, he was already at work on Psalm 134 in a four-part setting,[2] and many Italian songs also survive from this period.[3]

On May 8, 1811, Meyer Beer's first serious creation, an oratorio with soloists, chorus, and a full orchestra, *Gott und die Natur* (God and Nature), was performed with success in Berlin.

A fellow student at the Vogler school, although by a few years Beer's senior, was the soon-to-be famous Carl Maria von Weber (1786–1826). Together with a third budding composer, Johann Baptist Gänsbacher (1778–1844), they founded a society which they called Der Harmonischer Verein (The Society for Harmony), dedicated mainly to the renewal of German music. But the society also had a minor agenda of promoting its members' careers, via written reviews of each other's compositions.

---

2. Sketches for this work, dated Darmstadt May 30, 1810, are to be found in the Meyerbeer *Nachlass*, housed in the Staatsbibliothek zu Berlin. The author is indebted to Dr. Roland Schmidt-Hensel for allowing him to study these and several other important pieces in the collection.

3. Six of these songs, originally with a dedication to a certain Mademoiselle Beyme, were edited and published by Reiner Zimmermann in *Giacomo Meyerbeer: Lieder*, vol. 1, *1810–1839* (Leipzig: Edition Peters, 1982), 1–19, and may be heard on CDs. However, several others, unpublished (including "Ariette" and "Canzonette"), exist in the Meyerbeer *Nachlass*.

Meyerbeer and Weber, friends for life from Darmstadt onward, shown on two early twentieth-century cigarette cards in a series depicting famous composers (David Faiman collection)

Weber was a genuine nationalist, deeply concerned that no first-rate operas had been composed in the German language, other than a couple by Mozart and possibly Beethoven's *Leonora* (i.e., the original three-act version of *Fidelio*), if indeed it had yet been heard outside of French-occupied Vienna. Weber was quick to recognize his young colleague's genius and saw in him one of the potential rejuvenators of true German music. Beer, for his part, probably realized that membership in such a potentially prestigious society was important in that it might help him in the quest, which had eluded so many previous generations of his coreligionists, to gain acceptance into Prussian society.

On August 16, 1812, Meyer's beloved grandfather Liepmann Meyer Wulff died. Meyer was heartbroken. In a letter to his mother, he wrote:

> ... Yes, if Grandfather had even a glimmer of consciousness on his deathbed, it must have been a comfort to him to know that

his children will never leave the faith he so warmly embraced. Therefore, please accept a promise from me in his name that I will always live in the religion in which he died. I do not believe that there is any better way to honor his memory.

Please forgive me, but I am unable to write more today.

Farewell

Meyer B[4]

Thereafter, although he continued to use the name Meyer in letters to his father, for everyone else he joined the two names, creating Meyerbeer as a surname and adopting his father's given name, Jakob, as his own (alternatively, Jacques, when writing letters to French recipients, or Giacomo to Italians). In spite of the genuine sadness expressed in this letter to his mother, Meyerbeer had another reason for feeling the need to honor his grandfather, for the latter had settled upon him an endowment of a size that would enable him to devote all his efforts to his art without needing to depend on music in order to make a living.

Toward the end of his stay with Vogler, Meyer Beer composed his first opera, *Jephtas Gelübde* (Jephtha's Vow). It is based upon the biblical story of a daughter who had the misfortune to be the first person to come out of the house to greet her father, Jephtha, upon his triumphant return from war.[5] Unbeknownst to her, her father had vowed to sacrifice the first living creature he would encounter should he be successful in the battle. Beer twisted the original tragic tale in order to give it a happy ending. He also embellished the biblical story by adding some additional players and naming the unnamed characters, for in the Bible, Jephtha alone is named.

In his introduction to a recently published performing score of *Jephta*, Cambridge scholar Robert Letellier points out the underlying

---

4. Heinz Becker and Gudrun Becker, *Giacomo Meyerbeer: A Life in Letters*, trans. Mark Violette (Portland, OR: Amadeus Press, 1989), 25–26.

5. Judges, chapter 11.

Hebrew meanings of the various names that Beer chose for these characters: Sulima, Jephtha's daughter (associated with "peaceable"); Asmavett, her beloved (associated with "strong until death"); Abdon, the wicked rival of Asmavett (associated with "destruction"). Letellier might also have included the name of the remaining character, Tirza, Sulima's close friend (associated with "doing the will of her friend"). Although the significance of these names would probably have been lost on audiences at that time, one sees that the Hebrew lessons young Meyer had received from Wolfssohn had evidently made their mark. But more importantly, it is instructive that even in this early work, as was to be the case throughout his entire operatic career, Meyer Beer was deeply concerned with the question of right versus wrong – even at the heavenly level!

On December 23, 1812, *Jephtas Gelübde* received its first of three performances at Munich's Hofoper Theater, all conducted by the composer. Although his diary speaks of the rehearsals as having been beset with difficulties, Beer appears to have been happy with the end results, and the reviews were favorable.

Nevertheless, the opera vanished into obscurity until the German musicologist Edgar Istel published an extremely favorable analytic study early in the twentieth century.[6] Istel's analysis drew attention to a wealth of original and innovative features in this work, and to the remarkably high level of musical inspiration manifested by such a young composer. More recently, a full performing score was published by Robert Letellier and Mark Starr.[7] Furthermore, shortly

---

6. Edgar Istel. "Meyerbeer's Way to Mastership: Employment of the Modern Leading-Motive before Wagner's Birth," trans. Theodore Baker, *The Musical Quarterly* (January 1926):72–109, reprinted in Letellier, *Reader*, 268–94.
7. Robert Ignatius Letellier and Mark Starr, eds., *Giacomo Meyerbeer: Jephtas Gelübde (Jephtha's Vow) – Vocal/Piano Score* (Newcastle upon Tyne: Cambridge Scholars Publishing, 2013). Dr. Letellier had previously hunted

before this book went to press, conductor and musicologist Dario Salvi, together with a cast of equally fervent Meyerbeer enthusiasts, made a studio recording of this opera, complete with ballet music and spoken dialog, for the Naxos record company.

A fruitful source of material that Vogler had given his students was the collection of oriental fables known as *The Arabian Nights*. One of these formed the framework for Weber's opera *Abu Hasan*, and another for Meyerbeer's second opera, *Wirt und Gast, oder Aus Scherz Ernst* (Host and guest, or Taking a joke too seriously). The latter received its first performance in Stuttgart's Court Theater on January 6, 1813, barely two weeks after Munich had premiered his *Jephtha*. However, Meyerbeer was dissatisfied with the performances, and the public were not enthusiastic. He thereupon set about revising it and, as *Alimelek, oder Die beiden Kalifen* (Alimelek, or the Two caliphs), he took it to Vienna, where it was performed at the Kärntnertor Theater on October 20, 1814. There, he was to learn several unexpected lessons that were to serve him in good stead for the rest of his life.

The first lesson that Meyerbeer learned in Vienna was the importance of *timing*. In this respect, he could not have chosen a worse time to stage a new German-language opera in that city. For, only five months earlier, Vienna had witnessed the premiere of *Fidelio* by Beethoven (1770–1827) – a hard act for anyone to follow!

Secondly, following the exile of Napoleon,[8] the capital of the

---

down and studied the extant manuscripts of *Jephtas Gelübde*, part of a project to make manuscripts of all Meyerbeer's operas available to scholars, and which led inter alia to the monumental series: Richard Arsenty and Robert Letellier, *Giacomo Meyerbeer: The Complete Libretti in Five Volumes; In the Original and in English Translations* (London: Cambridge Scholars Press, 2004).

8. Napoleon abdicated on April 4, 1814, and was exiled to the Isle of Elba. Louis XVIII became king of France. Napoleon returned to power in March 1815 but was finally defeated at the Battle of Waterloo on June 18, 1815. While

Austro-Hungarian Empire was filling up with numerous heads of state who were gathering there for the Congress of Vienna (November 1, 1814–June 8, 1815), the aim of which was no less than to establish the borders of Europe, which were to remain more or less unchanged for the next hundred years. Most of the conference attendees accordingly had anything on their minds except music – as the following contemporary report illustrates:

> There was gold plate and many toasts and many songs recited by the artists of the Italian Opera. The Grand Duchess[9] at this repeated her remark that music always gave her nausea and asked the singers to stop; it was only with difficulty that they persuaded her to agree sulkily that "God Save the King" might be played after the royal toast.[10]

Worse still, for any serious music lovers, a repeat performance of *Fidelio*, under the baton of none other than its composer, had been scheduled for merely a week after *Alimelek*!

> On October 28 a performance was given of Beethoven's *Fidelio*; and on Tuesday, November 29, took place, in the presence of the Tsar and Frederick William III, a gala concert of Beethoven's music. The Seventh Symphony was given, followed by the piece which Beethoven had just written in celebration of Lord Wellington's victory at Vitoria. Beethoven, although by then completely deaf, conducted the latter composition; he stood there, among

---

in Vienna, Meyerbeer composed a short opera, *Das Brandenburger Tor* (The Brandenburg Gate) in honor of Prussia's part in the defeat of Napoleon. It was scheduled for performance in Berlin in August 1815, but it arrived there after the king had left for the Vienna Congress and was never performed during its composer's lifetime.

9. This was Grand Duchess Catherine Pavlovna of Russia (1788–1819).
10. Harold Nicolson, *The Congress of Vienna: A Study of Allied Unity, 1812–1822* (New York: Harcourt, Brace, 1946), 116.

that distinguished but unappreciative audience, a "short and stout" figure waving his baton triumphantly.[11]

And who, would you guess, played the timpani – amid what must surely have been quite a confused din – in that orchestra "conducted" by the deaf Beethoven?

You guessed correctly – Jakob Meyerbeer!

Nevertheless, Weber was much impressed with his friend's new opera, conducting it first in Prague, where he was director of the opera, and later, in 1820, in Dresden after he had become director of that city's opera. However, we do not need to rely solely upon Weber's opinion, because, there is now a published score of Meyerbeer's second opera.[12] Furthermore, thanks to the efforts of its editor, Volker Tosta, a stage performance, which was recorded,[13] was mounted at Bad Urach in 2010, as a double bill with Weber's *Abu Hasan*, and a full studio recording is planned by Naxos under the baton of Dario Salvi.[14]

After *Alimelek*, Meyerbeer stayed on in Vienna, giving concerts – for he was still a greatly admired piano virtuoso – and in order to try to take some composition lessons from the aged Antonio Salieri (1750–1825). The latter was the composer of nearly forty operas and the much-respected director of the orchestra at the Imperial Chapel. Today, Salieri is mainly remembered for the claim, made in his dotage, that he had killed Mozart. In 1815, however, the imperial Kapellmeister was impressed with Meyerbeer's two opera scores and overall musicianship.

---

11. Nicolson, *The Congress of Vienna*, 161.
12. Volker Tosta, ed., *Giacomo Meyerbeer: Alimelek oder Wirt und Gast – Vocal and Orchestral Score* (Stuttgart: Edition Nordstern, 2011).
13. *Giacomo Meyerbeer: Alimelek oder Wirt und Gast* (CPO Records [to be released]).
14. Dario Salvi, private communication to the author, January 30, 2020.

The composer Antonio Salieri (1750–1825), who recommended that Meyerbeer compose operas to Italian rather than German texts, painted by Joseph Willibrord Mähler, 1815 (Wikimedia Commons)

The only advice Salieri is said to have been willing to give his young colleague was that he should stop using that most unmusical language, German, for his operas, and betake himself to Italy, the land where opera had been born.

And so, after some further concertizing that brought him inter alia to Paris and London, in 1816 Meyerbeer took Salieri's advice and went to Italy.

Chapter 3

The Land Where Lemons Blossom

Meyerbeer, like so many German composers before and after, became enchanted with Italy. His first visit there was in 1816. However, prompted by Salieri, he embarked upon a study tour in that country that was to last nine years (including a number of trips home) and boost him to world prominence. In Sicily he collected ancient folk melodies. In Verona he met up with two of his old friends, the famous clarinetist Heinrich Joseph Baermann (1784–1847) and the latter's partner, the soprano Hélène Harlas (1785–1818), who had performed the role of Sulima in the Munich production of his *Jephtas Gelübde*. In their honor he composed a playful new work for chorus and orchestra, *Gli amori di Teolinda* (The loves of Theolinda), featuring his two friends as soloists.[1]

According to letters received regularly by his family, Meyerbeer was absolutely enchanted by the place – a country in which he was happy to be regarded as a *German* composer. However, he could not forget Salieri's admonishment that his previous operas had been too

---

1. For example, *Giacomo Meyerbeer: Gli Amore di Teolinda* (Orfeo C 054-831 A [one CD]).

serious and that he should stop using German texts. He continued his study of the Italian language with the same kind of determination that he applied to all of his studies and which he would later apply to the French language.

Gioacchino Rossini (1792–1868), one year his junior, was Italy's rising star. So Giacomo (as Jakob took to calling himself) set about the detailed study of his young contemporary's latest operas. After he had grasped the essentials, he tried his own hand at an Italian opera, à la Rossini. His librettist was Gaetano Rossi (1774–1855), who had already written the libretti for several successful operas by other composers and whose services Meyerbeer would again turn to several times during his budding operatic career. Their first collaboration resulted in *Romilda e Costanza* (Romilda and Costanza), which had its premiere on July 19, 1817, at the Teatro Nuovo in Padua.

Padua's Teatro Verdi, formerly Teatro Nuovo, where Meyerbeer's Romilda e Costanza *received its world premiere (David Faiman collection)*

The opera's complex plot is one of love, rivalry, royalty, loyalty, treachery, and – surprisingly for all concerned – a happy ending. The two ladies named in the opera's title are both in love with the same man, who once loved one but now loves the other. Perhaps Meyerbeer's idea of a happy ending was a bit far-fetched, but to his unexpected delight, the opera was a stunning success, in every way.

The cast was perfect, the famous publishing house of Riccordi printed extracts that were quickly snapped up by an eager public that, most importantly, loved the work. Equally amazing was the fact that Giacomo actually received a *commission* (his very first!) to write another opera. Old Salieri's advice had indeed proved sound.

The complete *Romilda e Costanza* had not yet been recorded at the time of this writing. However, one extract, the trio "Che barbaro tormento!" (What cruel torment!) is included in the Opera Rara CD, *Meyerbeer in Italy*,[2] and a performing score has been prepared by Robert Letellier and Dario Salvi. Moreover, a performance took place at Bad Wildbad in July 2019, which will hopefully be issued in CD format.

The success of *Romilda e Costanza* was the first of what were to be many such occasions in which this basically modest man was to worry about how to ensure that his next opera would not fall short of expectations. His formula was ever more diligent study and hard work. In the present situation he kept Italy waiting for two years before staging *Semiramide riconosciuta* (Semiramis recognized), which relates an even more complex tale of love, sexual confusion, and attempted murder, set in ancient Babylon. It was premiered on February 3, 1819, this time at the Teatro Regio in Turin. For its libretto Meyerbeer resorted to a much-used text by the poet Pietro Metastasio (1698–1782), because such was the taste of that

---

2. *Meyerbeer in Italy* (Opera Rara ORR222 [one CD]).

city. Some scholars have suggested that his friend Rossi may have helped Meyerbeer bring the libretto up to date, but be that as it may, Meyerbeer was full of foreboding over the opera's reception. It turned out that he needn't have worried, as once again his composition was a stunning success. Royalty, in the shape of the king and queen of Sardinia,[3] were in attendance, and according to a letter he wrote home, they presented him with a ring.

Eighteenth-century painting by Pietro Domenico Oliviero of Turin's Teatro Regio (later destroyed by fire), where Meyerbeer's Semiramide riconosciuta *was premiered (Wikimedia Commons)*

---

3. King Victor Emanuel I and Queen Maria Theresa.

Semiramide riconosciuta represented an interesting turning point in the relationship between Meyerbeer and Rossini, who was subsequently to become his lifelong friend. For if hitherto the latter had been a role model for Meyerbeer's Italian operas, this second of his operas was the first to have an influence on his Italian friend. This became evident a few years later when Rossini was himself to compose a *Semiramide*, and his librettist, none other than Rossi, was to provide him with, in his own words, an *"introduzione alla Meyerbeer"*![4]

Semiramide riconosciuta has enjoyed two contemporary revivals, both of which were recorded.[5] This gives modern listeners an opportunity both to enjoy this work afresh and also to make comparisons with Rossini's *Semiramide* – which has remained in the operatic repertory ever since it was originally composed and of which several recordings exist.

Actually, the commission that Meyerbeer had originally received for his first opera had initially come from Venice. However, the theater manager there demanded what Meyerbeer considered to be an outrageously high prepayment as insurance from someone who, after all, was not yet a famous composer. For that reason, its premiere took place in nearby Padua. Nevertheless, Venice was one of the cities that staged subsequent performances of *Romilda e Costanza*, and it did not repeat its initial slight when Meyerbeer's third Italian opera, *Emma di Resburgo* (Emma of Roxburgh), set in the Scottish Highlands, premiered on June 26, 1819, at Venice's Teatro San Benedetto.

---

4. The similarities between the *Semiramide* of Rossini and the earlier one of Meyerbeer are discussed in Robert Ignatius Letellier, *An Introduction to the Dramatic Works of Giacomo Meyerbeer: Operas, Ballets, Cantatas, Plays* (Aldershot, UK: Ashgate Publishing, 2008), 59.
5. Meyerbeer: Semiramide (Naxos 8.660205–06 [two CDs]); Meyerbeer: Semiramide (Dynamic CDS 533/1–2. [two CDs]).

Emma di Resburgo, with a libretto by Rossi, turned out to be a milestone in Meyerbeer's operatic career. To say that it was an even greater success in Italy than were its two predecessors would be correct, but somewhat tame. For, in its first year, it received over seventy performances in Venice alone, and was successfully performed all over the country. However, a more significant sign of its worth was that it was performed outside of Italy, including in his native Germany and in Austria.

Meyerbeer himself was not so happy to have these works, "my wild oats," as he later called his Italian operas, performed in Germany. In particular, they were composed for the Italian language, and to suit a long tradition of what Italians expected of "their" opera. By contrast, the German language lacks the lyrical flow of Italian, causing any translation (e.g., the mere title, *Emma von Roxburg*) to result in something that is both awkward to sing and alien to the more serious German tastes. Beethoven's *Fidelio*, for example, contains wonderful music but, as everyone was (and still is) quick to acknowledge, a plot celebrating marital fidelity is not exactly the stuff of which opera is usually made! Furthermore, gaps in *Fidelio*'s musical flow, into which spoken text is inserted – following the German *Singspiel* tradition – are often a major impediment to dramatic production.

Thus, Meyerbeer's success in Italy was, for his fellow Germans, on the one hand, a credit to the creative power of their country, but also a disgrace to their (self-proclaimed) superior artistic principles on which the composer had been raised.

Nevertheless, in Dresden, Carl Maria von Weber, although in the forefront of the debate at that time over where opera should be going, gave German audiences the opportunity to hear his friend's *Emma di Resburgo*, in its original Italian language. He even kept it in repertory from 1820 to 1824. However, in order to wash out their ears, as it were, he also offered his local audiences Meyerbeer's older, German-language opera, *Wirt und Gast,* in its revised form as *Alimelek*.

In recent years *Emma di Resburgo* received a concert performance in Vienna, which was broadcast and of which a recording was issued.[6]

Meyerbeer had, by now, become an opera composer of some standing, *Emma di Resburgo* having even upstaged Rossini's latest premiere *Edoardo e Cristina*! It is therefore not surprising that his next two commissions came from none other than Italy's foremost opera house, then as now – La Scala, Milan.

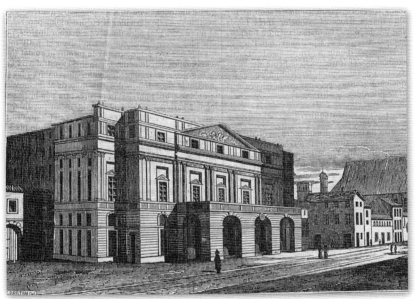

Old engraving depicting the La Scala opera house, Milan, where Meyerbeer's Margherita d'Anjou *was premiered (David Faiman collection)*

The first of Meyerbeer's operas for La Scala premiered on November 14, 1820. It was *Margherita d'Anjou* (Margaret of Anjou). It has a semi-fictitious plot around the widow of England's King Henry VI, returning from France with their infant son, in order to claim the throne of England for him. It uses a libretto by Felice Romani

---

6. *Giacomo Meyerbeer: Emma di Resburgo* (Newplay NE003 [two CDs]).

(1788–1865). Interestingly, although the opera was in two acts in Italian, Romani based his plot upon an original three-act French play, a so-called "mélodrame historique" by the eminent French playwright Guilbert-René-Charles de Pixérécourt (1773–1844). We shall meet M. Pixérécourt again in the next chapter.

Opera Rara has produced a very fine recording of *Margherita d'Anjou*.[7] When Opera Rara recorded this work, they organized a concert performance at the Royal Festival Hall, which the present author and his wife were fortunate enough to be able to attend. Upon hearing forgotten classics for the first time, one automatically makes comparisons: an extended violin solo that could have come straight from the pen of Paganini; and an act 1 aria, "Per noi di Gloria già splende un raggio" (A ray of glory is already shining for us), which, musically, is astonishingly reminiscent of "Ah! Non giunge uman pensiero" (Human thought cannot comprehend), the closing aria from the well-known opera *La Sonnambula* of Vincenzo Bellini (1801–1835). Interestingly, the latter was written a full eleven years after *Margherita d'Anjou* had begun its successful career. So here was the Italian Bellini paying tribute to his by then illustrious Prussian contemporary.

Meyerbeer's fifth Italian opera – his second for La Scala – was *L'Esule di Granata* (The exile from Granada), with a text by Romani. It is set in fifteenth-century Granada and presents us with something of a mystery: its premiere took place on March 12, 1822, but there were very few subsequent performances. Why? Moreover, unlike its predecessors, it did not spread all over Italy and the rest of the world. In fact, the only other documented production took place four years later in Florence. Why? Opera Rara devoted an entire CD to extracts from this work,[8] from which it may be judged to be a fully mature opera, both musically and dramatically.

---

7. Meyerbeer: *Margherita d'Anjou* (Opera Rara ORC25 [three CDs]).
8. Meyerbeer: *L'Esule di Granata* (Opera Rara ORR234 [one CD]).

The musicologist Jennifer Jackson has suggested that coming at the very end of La Scala's 1821–22 season, before the Lent break, may have accounted for *L'Esule*'s short run at that theater.[9] And, moreover, because Meyerbeer subsequently recycled parts of its music for his next opera,[10] he himself may not have wanted it to continue in the repertory. The first part of her conjecture is plausible. However, by this time, Giacomo Meyerbeer was famous all over Italy, not to mention the rest of the world. Theater managers would surely have been eager to stage this latest work from the pen of their amazing "Tedesco" (Italian for "German"). Florence did. So why not the others? There would appear to be no satisfactory answer to this mystery.

A possibly related mystery is the fate of another Meyerbeer opera, *Alamanzor*, to a text by Rossi, which was advertised at that time but never performed. No score of *Almanzor* has ever come to light and most scholars tend to believe that it was an earlier form of what eventually became *L'Esule di Granata*, mainly because Almanzor is the principal character in the latter. However, as tidy as this theory may seem, it has several problems, not least of which is the apparent change of librettist! Most seriously, perhaps, is the entry for October 31, 1843, in Meyerbeer's diary. It reads, in typically terse items:

> At 12 Kastner. The list of my operas for the médailleur Borel. Portrait for the Biographie de Contemporaines.[11]

What precisely Meyerbeer discussed with the composer Jean-Georges Kastner (1810–1867), and which particular portrait he gave to the book publishers are of no relevance to the present discussion.

---

9. Jennifer Jackson, personal communication, January 7, 2013.
10. George Loomis, program notes to the Opera Rara recording of *L'Esule di Granata* (Opera Rara ORR234 [one CD]), 27.
11. English translation by Robert Letellier, *The Diaries of Giacomo Meyerbeer*, vol. 2, 81.

However the list of operas Meyerbeer states that he gave to Borrel is most revealing.[12] The present author was fortunate to find one of these medallions, and the list on its reverse side plainly reads:

> Jephta. Alimeleck
> Brandenburger Tor
> Semiramide Reconoscinta. Emma
> Margherita d'Anjou. Romilda e Costanza
> Almanzor. Esale di Granata
> Crociato. Robert le Diable
> Les Huguenots. Le Prophète. L'Étoile du Nord

Would the by-then famous Meyerbeer have needed to "pad" his publication list? Or, could Borrel have added *Almanzor*, thinking that the busy composer had forgotten to mention it? If the engraved list was indeed unedited, then this mention of both *Almanzor* and *L'Esale* (sic) *di Granata* could indicate that Meyerbeer himself was under the impression that by 1843 he had written seven Italian operas. So perhaps one day a manuscript of *Almanzor* will be found.

The Borrel medallion, with its list of Meyerbeer operas provided by the composer (David Faiman collection)

---

12. Alfred Borrel (1836–1927) was a celebrated medalist who had learned his profession from his father. His products bear the signature "Borrel," or "Borrel F." (Fils) or "Borrel xxxx," with the year the medal was struck. Note that Meyerbeer wrote the name with a single *r*.

After *L'Esule di Granata*, Meyerbeer made a brief trip home to Berlin in order to see his family and friends. In one of his letters, the composer Carl Maria von Weber wrote:

> Last Friday I had the joy of having Meyerbeer spend a whole day with me. It was a truly happy day – a reminder of the good times in Mannheim. We did not part until midnight. Meyerbeer is going to Trieste to produce his *Crociato*. Next year he returns to Berlin where he will perhaps write a German opera. Heaven grant it! I have made many appeals to his conscience.[13]

Robert Letellier mentions that during this trip, Meyerbeer tried, unsuccessfully, to secure a performance of his German-language opera, *Das Brandenburger Tor* (The Brandenburg Gate), which is listed on the Borrel medallion.[14]

For what was to be Meyerbeer's final Italian-language opera, *Il Crociato in Egitto* (The Crusader in Egypt), the composer returned to Venice, to the Teatro La Fenice, the city's principal opera house. The premiere took place there on March 7, 1824.

Like his first Italian opera, *Il Crociato* includes a love story involving one man and two rival women. It is set in Egypt during the sixth Crusade. However, it is on an altogether grander scale than *Romilda e Costanze*. Instead of the former's Greek-style chorus, whose function is merely to keep the audience informed as to what is going on, in *Il Crociato*, the chorus forms a major part of the action, as do two on-stage bands.

Not surprisingly, *Il Crociato in Egitto* quickly became an

---

13. English translation by Robert Letellier, *The Diaries of Giacomo Meyerbeer*, vol. 1, 377n326.
14. English translation by Robert Letellier, *The Diaries of Giacomo Meyerbeer*, vol. 1, 377n326.

Old postcard depicting the interior of La Fenice, Venice, where Meyerbeer's Il Crociato in Egitto *premiered (David Faiman collection)*

international success. From the full recording that has been issued by Opera Rara,[15] one can easily discern musical ideas that were to inspire both Meyerbeer and other famous composers for several generations. Just one example of its influence was a soprano aria that Bellini composed for insertion by his friend Amalie Hähnel (1807–1849) into the 1829 Vienna production of Meyerbeer's work. The diva evidently did not consider the original opera to contain sufficient numbers to give maximum expression to her talents! And Bellini, as we saw in our discussion of *Margherita d'Anjou*, was not one to ignore the talents of his Prussian contemporary.

For the London performance of *Il Crociato in Egitto*, which took place in 1825, Meyerbeer was too busy to attend in person. So he sent over his good friend, Giovanni Battista Velluti (1780–1861) – better known as one of the last of the genuine *castrato* singers – to oversee and conduct the production. Meyerbeer had composed the role of

---

15. *Meyerbeer: Il Crociato in Egitto* (Opera Rara ORC10 [three CDs]).

Armando especially for Velluti, who performed it with much success in Italy. However, with the passing of the era of *castrati*, the part of Armando came to be performed by a female soprano. Accordingly, for the London production, Velluti coached the soprano Maria Felicia Malibran (1808–1836) to sing the role. Writing in 1848, the music critic Charles Grüneisen quotes the following from an anonymous review of the London production for the *Quarterly Musical Magazine and Review* of 1825:

> ... But if a man writes the fullness of the German harmony with the grace of the Italian melody – if he collects the expedients which are scattered here and there, and uses them to new and better purposes and effects – if he accumulates imagery – introduces unexpected, bold, and beautiful transitions, converts an ornament into an exclamation of passion, or gives an outline a singer of expression fills up magnificently – the man who does all this, at this time of day, we say must be considered as an original and highly-gifted genius: and such we esteem Meyerbeer. In drawing our definition, we have, indeed, only recapitulated the qualities which appear to us to be compacted in *Il Crociato in Egitto*. Beautiful traits of melody, rich harmony, novel and grand effects, intense feeling, and passionate expression, are all brought together with a fine vein of imagination. Solidity, energy, and pathos are compounded, and employed with great delicacy and force as to the means by turns and in season. Above all, he has a vivid perception of the beautiful and the great, unalloyed by false notions of effect....[16]

In fact, so "grand" was *Il Crociato* seen to be that even Paris, the home of "Grande Opéra," demanded it, and they insisted that the

---

16. Charles Grüneisen, *Memoir of Meyerbeer, with Notices, Historical and Critical, of His Celebrated Operas* (1848), reproduced in Letellier, *Reader*, 82–83.

maestro himself come over to oversee and conduct the production in 1825. A consequent invitation to compose an opera for that city led to Meyerbeer transferring his base from Italy to Paris – a lifelong dream that had finally come true.

Chapter 4
Paris at Last!

Meyerbeer's arrival in Paris was a bit like a game of musical chairs with Rossini, who by this time was a friendly rival. We already saw how Rossini had been inspired for his own *Semiramide* (which premiered at La Fenice, Venice, on February 3, 1823) by Meyerbeer's earlier opera of that name. However, *Semiramide* was to be Rossini's last opera for an Italian opera house. Thereafter, he moved his base to Paris, where he became musical director of the city's Théâtre Royal Italien ("Théâtre Italien" for short). It was there that his next opera, *Il viaggio a Reims* (The journey to Reims), received its premiere on June 19, 1825. In the meantime, as we saw in the previous chapter, Meyerbeer had scored an enormous success all over Italy with *Il Crociato in Egitto*, which, like Rossini's *Semiramide*, also had its premiere at Venice's La Fenice opera house. So it is perhaps not too surprising that Rossini lost no time in inviting his friend to Paris to perform *Il Crociato in Egitto* there. The premiere took place on September 25, 1825, at the Salle Louvois, a venue that had been occupied by the Théâtre Italien for the past six years. This timing was slightly unfortunate for Meyerbeer because, although *Il Crociato in Egitto* was successful with the French public, there was only time for six performances before the Théâtre Italien had to move house yet again, this time to the Salle Favart. The company moved its location no fewer than nine times during the nineteenth century, and to Meyerbeer's misfortune, its latest move occurred on November 8, 1825.

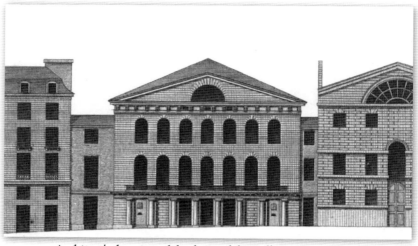

Architect's drawing of the facia of the Salle Louvois, where Il Crociato in Egitto *received its Paris premiere on September 25, 1825 (Wikimedia Commons)*

One might suppose that performances could have resumed at the Salle Favart, to which the company moved. But such an assumption would ignore the immense lengths to which Meyerbeer always went in supervising all aspects of every production. Of such efforts one of his contemporaries wrote thus:

> Never will we know the true cost of rehearsals to Meyerbeer in terms of insomnia, anxiety, fear, work, and despair. He saw everything, he thought of everything, he supervised everything: libretto, music, staging, scenery, costumes, songs, and dancing.[1]

---

1. Charles de Boigne, *Petits mémoires de l'Opéra* (Paris : Librairie Nouvelle, 1857), 12, cited in Patrick Barbier, *Opera in Paris, 1800–1850 : A Lively History*,

Clearly such a person could not simply move a production from one house to another with a different stage and facilities. Nevertheless, plans were made for a Paris revival of *Il Crociato* in the future.

At the personal level, 1825 was both a hectic and a sad year for Meyerbeer because in October his beloved father, Jacob Herz Beer, died. At the time, Meyerbeer was in Italy, where he had gone as soon as the French season of *Il Crociato* closed. So he did not reach Berlin in time for the funeral. Nevertheless, in November, before leaving Berlin, he became engaged to his cousin Minna Mosson.[2]

In the meantime, work had been in progress back in Paris to translate his *Margherita d'Anjou* into French, for performance at the Théâtre Royal de l'Odéon (l'Odéon, for short). As it happens, at the same time he had been negotiating with the Théâtre Italien management for a staging of *Il Crociato in Egitto* at their theater, he had also been in contact with the Odéon management to produce a French-language version of *Margherita d'Anjou* for performance at their theater.

Why a French translation? Because there were strict rules about the format of operas that could be performed at each of Paris's four major opera houses.[3] The Théâtre Italien, as its name implies, performed only foreign operas, in the Italian language, so *Il Crociato* could be performed there as is. The Odéon, on the other hand, was also permitted to perform foreign operas, but only if translated into French. However, Meyerbeer faced an additional complication: the author of the drama on which this opera was based, R.C.G. de

---

trans. Robert Luoma (Portland, OR: Amadeus Press, 1995), 56; used with permission of Rowman and Littlefield.

2. Meyerbeer's wife Minna (1804–1886) was the daughter of Grandfather Wulff's eldest daughter Hanka (1770–1847), who had adopted the name Jeanette.

3. See for example Mark Everist, *Music Drama at the Paris Odéon, 1824–1828* (Berkeley: University of California Press, 2002).

Pixérécourt, was annoyed that Meyerbeer's original librettist, Felice Romani, had ruthlessly cut out the middle act of his three-act *mélodrame*, *Marguerite d'Anjou*, in order to produce a two-act Italian opera. Pixérécourt insisted that for the French version of the opera, the original three-act format be restored.

This obviously required an enormous amount of extra effort on Meyerbeer's part, aided to a great extent by the librettist and writer Thomas-Maria-François Sauvage (1794–1877). Not only did the plot of the opera need stretching, but additional music was necessary. For this purpose Meyerbeer took advantage of the fact that his *Emma di Resburgo* had never been performed in Paris. *Emma*, accordingly, became the musical source for the newly inserted act 2, act 1 being essentially a French retranslation of the original Italian act 1 (but with the overture of *Emma* replacing the overture to the Italian *Margherita*);[4] act 2 of the Italian version, after retranslation back into French, now became act 3.

The appropriately renamed *Marguerite d'Anjou* (Margaret's name now being written in French instead of Italian) premiered at the Odéon on March 11, 1826, again to enormous public acclaim. It actually enjoyed far more performances in Paris than had *Il Crociato in Egitto*, owing to the forced closure of the Salle Louvois, where the latter had started its short run.

But Meyerbeer, ever on the move, was in Berlin to marry Minna on May 25, 1826, and back in Paris three days later, with his new bride in tow, in order to work on yet another project for the Odéon.[5] This was to be called *La Nymphe du Danube* (The nymph of the

---

4. This simplification only outlines the main differences between the Italian *Margherita d'Anjou* and the French *Marguerite d'Anjou*. A detailed discussion may be found in Everist, *Giacomo Meyerbeer and Music Drama*, 146–56.

5. A year-by-year outline of Meyerbeer's travels during this period is given in Letellier, *The Diaries of Giacomo Meyerbeer*, vol. 1, 385ff.

Old engraving of L'Odéon, where the French-language, extended version of Meyerbeer's Margherita d'Anjou *was first staged (David Faiman collection)*

Danube) – using a pastiche of music drawn from all of his Italian operas.[6] This was not Meyerbeer's first experience with the pastiche form of entertainment, because in June of that year, the Odéon staged *La Fausse Agnès*, which had been cobbled together by the music critic Castil-Blaze (1784–1857), employing the overture from Meyerbeer's *Romilda e Costanza* as its own, together with arias set to music by a variety of other composers.

Although Meyerbeer completed *La Nymphe du Danube*, it was never performed because even though the Odéon had plans to stage three pastiches that season– *La Nymphe*, Rossini's *Ivanhoé*

---

6. For a detailed discussion of the pastiches at the Odéon, see Everist, *Music Drama at the Paris Odeon*, 171ff.

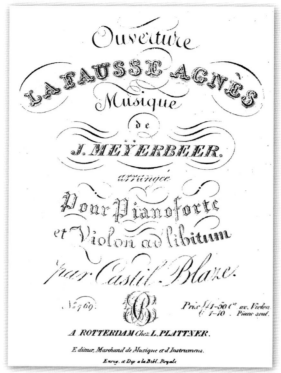

The overture to Castil-Blaze's pastiche, La Fausse Agnès, *originally composed by Meyerbeer for his own* Romilda e Costanza *and recycled for his* Semiramide riconosciuta (David Faiman collection)

(Ivanhoe), and Weber's *Les Bohémiens* (The Bohemians) – there were rehearsal problems, and only Rossini's and Weber's works were actually staged.

However, with successes at both the Théâtre Italien and the Odéon behind him, Meyerbeer next turned his attention to a third Paris theater, the Opéra-Comique, of which none other than Pixérécourt happened to be the director. Together with librettists Germain Delavigne (1790–1868) and Augustin-Eugène Scribe (1791–1861), Meyerbeer started work on a three-act *opéra-comique*

The Berlin graves of Eugenie and Alfred, Meyerbeer's two children who died in infancy (photograph by David Faiman)

to be called *Robert le Diable* (Robert the devil). Like the other two opera houses we have already encountered, the Opéra-Comique also had its rules. Its productions had to be in French – but original French-language creations, not translations. According to research by Everist,[7] *Robert le Diable* was almost completely ready for the Opéra-Comique when two complications occurred: Pixérécourt resigned his directorship of the theater at the end of August 1827; and on December 9 that year, tragedy struck Meyerbeer – his baby daughter, Eugenie, who was not yet four months old, died.

Not surprisingly, Meyerbeer spent most of 1828 back in Berlin

---

7. Everist, *Giacomo Meyerbeer and Music Drama*, 177–214.

with Minna, but during that time, his *Il Crociato in Egitto* was revived in Paris, and on October 31, a son, Alfred, was born. But tragedy struck yet again on April 13, 1829, when after less than six months of life, little Alfred also passed away.

After taking Minna for a cure at Baden-Baden, where she gave birth to their daughter Blanca in July 1830, Meyerbeer resumed his travels and was back in Paris in August to begin a reworking of *Robert le Diable*.

With new, less than cooperative management at the Opéra-Comique, Meyerbeer and Scribe decided to move this first French-language joint creation to the fourth and grandest of Paris's four opera houses: L'Académie-Royal de Musique, simply referred to as "L'Opéra."

The Opéra had an enormous stage, equipped with the most advanced machinery for effecting scene changes, a magnificent corps de ballet, and an orchestra that was the envy of all visiting musicians.

Not surprisingly, for this house too there were strict rules. The

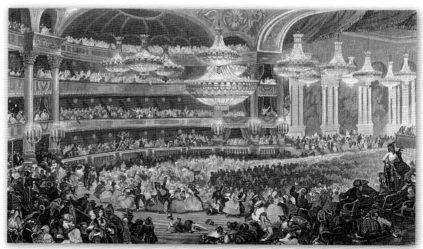

An 1847 engraving of L'Académie-Royal de Musique, "L'Opéra" (David Faiman collection)

Opéra was reserved for dramatic works in the French language, and, in the case of operas, with all spoken words set to music. Furthermore, operas there were required to be in five acts with a ballet in act 3.

However, the path to the Opéra was not to be straightforward. For it was at that theater that Meyerbeer began to appreciate something of the complexity of French politics and its effect on opera.

To recap the political situation in France at that time, we recall that Meyerbeer had been in Vienna in 1815 during the Congress of Vienna, which had reshaped Europe after the collapse of the Napoleonic Empire. Louis XVIII subsequently ruled France from 1815 to 1824, followed by his brother, Charles X, from 1824 to 1830, the two of them inaugurating a period of increasing social unrest. This was the period of Meyerbeer's first success in Paris. However, Charles was forced into exile as a result of a second revolution, the so-called "July Revolution" in 1830, which resulted in Louis Philippe wearing the crown until 1848, when revolutions broke out all over Europe.

Aiming at the Opéra, Delavigne helped Scribe and Meyerbeer to expand *Robert le Diable* into a five-act so-called *"grand opéra."* Meyerbeer naturally composed a ballet for the third act, as convention required for this theater, but as an innovation integrated it into the opera's plot. He signed a contract for *Robert le Diable* with the Opéra in 1829, but the opera's production was delayed by the 1830 July Revolution and the subsequent appointment of Louis-Désiré Véron (1798–1867) as new director of the opera house. Véron wanted to breathe new life into this austere institution and decided to spare no expense in making *Robert* a huge success. Elaborate scene painters were engaged, all of the most technologically up-to-date special effects were to be included, and of course, the splendid orchestra and corps de ballet were put at Meyerbeer's disposal. *Robert le Diable* premiered on November 21, 1831, producing a success the like of which that theater had never known. A firsthand description of the overall effect was given by the young Frédéric Chopin (1810–1849), newly arrived in Paris:

> I don't know whether there has ever been such magnificence in a theatre, whether it has ever before attained to the pomp of the new 5-act opera, "Robert le Diable," by Mayerbeer, who wrote Crociato – It is a masterpiece of the new school, in which devils (huge choirs) sing through speaking-trumpets, and souls rise from graves (but not, as in The Charlatan,[8] just in groups of 50 or 60); in which there is a diorama in the theatre, in which at the end you see the *intérieur* of a church, the whole church, at Christmas or Easter, lighted up, with monks, and all the congregation on the benches, and censors [sic]: – even with the organ, the sound of which on the stage is enchanting and amazing, also it nearly drowns the orchestra; nothing of the sort could be put on anywhere else. Meyerbeer has immortalized himself![9]

With sounds of *Robert le Diable* still singing in his inner ear, Chopin recorded his musical impressions of the opera in the *Duo concertant* in E Major, which he composed for cello and piano in collaboration with his cellist friend August-Joseph Franchomme (1808–1884). Moreover, it is probable that one or more of his solo piano works composed around 1831 were also inspired by *Robert le Diable*.[10]

It was not only Chopin who was impressed. Another famous composer who set down his musical impressions, as *Reminiscences of*

---

8. Chopin refers here to *The Charlatan, or the Raising of the Dead*, an 1814 opera in two acts by the long-forgotten Polish composer Karol Kurpinski (1785–1857). This (for us) unknown opera would evidently have been familiar to his Polish reader.

9. *Frederic Chopin: Chopin's Letters*, ed. Henryk Opienski, trans. E.L. Voynich (New York: Dover, 1988), 157.

10. Letellier, *The Diaries of Giacomo Meyerbeer*, vol. 1, 114. Here Letellier refers to the *Ballade* no. 2 in F Major, op. 38, which shows some resemblance to Alice's act 1 aria "Va, dit-elle."

Composer Frédéric Chopin (1810–1849), some of whose music was influenced by Meyerbeer's opera Robert le Diable, *photographed by Louis-Auguste Bisson, 1849 (Wikimedia Commons)*

Robert le Diable for solo piano, was Franz Liszt (1811–1886). Moreover the "Bertram" signature tune from this latest Meyerbeer opera provides the opening notes of Mendelssohn's second piano concerto.

The effect of *Robert le Diable* also continued to be felt in the music of later generations. Violeta's famous aria "Ah, fors'è lui che l'anima" (Ah, perhaps he is the one) in act 1 of *La Traviata* by Giuseppe Verdi (1813–1901) bears more than a casual resemblance – in melody, structure, and even words – to Meyerbeer's famous act 4 cavatina: "Robert, toi que j'aime" (Robert, it is you whom I love). And Verdi's opera was premiered twenty-two years after *Robert le Diable*!

Even the young Richard Wagner (1813–1883) wrote, regarding religion: "This son of Germany has taught us how it may be preached from the stage of a theatre."[11] Indeed Wagner appears to have internalized *Robert le Diable* to such an extent that at the end of his life, many of the effects, together with its underlying theme of religious unity, reappear, albeit grossly distorted, in the guise of the opera *Parsifal*[12] – Wagner's own subsequent attempt to preach religion from the stage of a theater!

So powerful was the effect of *Robert le Diable* on all who saw any of its enormous run of productions (the Opéra, alone, had staged 754 performances by 1893), that its influence reached well beyond the world of music. Honoré de Balzac (1799–1860) wrote an entire novelette, *Gambara*, about a young composer and the stunning effect of its hero's first encounter with a performance of Meyerbeer's opera:

> "Silence, my friend!" cried Gambara. "I am still under the spell of that glorious chorus of hell, made still more terrible by the long trumpets, – a new method of instrumentation. The broken cadenzas which give such force to Robert's scene, the cavatina in the fourth act, the finale of the first, all hold me in the grip of a supernatural power. No, not even Gluck's declamation ever produced so prodigious an effect, and I am amazed by such skill and learning."[13]

Alexandre Dumas (père; 1802–1870) set an entire short story, "Robert le Diable," chapter 53 of *The Count of Monte Cristo*, in the four intervals between the acts at a performance staged at the Opéra:

---

11. Quoted by Camile Bellaigue in *Portraits and Silhouettes of Musicians*, trans. Ellen Orr (New York: Dodd, Mead, 1897), 296.
12. See for example Walter Keller, *Wagner* 13, no. 2 (May 1992): 83–90.
13. Honoré de Balzac, *Gambara*, trans. Clara Bell and James Waring (Project Gutenberg ebook #1873), 31, https://www.gutenberg.org/files/1873/1873-h/1873-h.htm.

The pretext of an opera engagement was so much the more feasible, as there chanced to be on that very night a more than ordinary attraction at the Academie Royale. Levasseur, who had been suffering under severe illness, made his reappearance in the character of Bertrand, and, as usual, the announcement of the most admired production of the favorite composer of the day had attracted a brilliant and fashionable audience.[14]

In contemporary poetry too, *Robert le Diable* had its effect. Heinrich Heine (1797–1856), who was living in Paris at the time, includes, in his sarcastic love poem *Angelique*, the lines:

> *Wenn ich Billette bekommen kann,*
> *Bin ich sogar kapabel*
> *Dich in die Oper zu führen alsdann:*
> *Man gibt Robert-le-Diable.*
>
> *Es is ein grosses Zauberstück*
> *Voll Teufelslust und Liebe;*
> *Von Meyerbeer ist die Musik,*
> *Der schlechte Text von Scribe.*
>
> If I can get the tickets, then
> I promise we'll be going
> To see the opera again –
> Robert the Devil is showing.
>
> It's full of devlish lust galore
> And love in high falsetto;
> Meyerbeer composed the score
> To Scribë's vile libretto.[15]

---

14. Alexandre Dumas, *The Count of Monte Cristo* (Ware, Herts, UK: Wordsworth Classics, 1997), 430–41.
15. Heinrich Heine, "Angelique." English translation comes from Hal Draper, *The Complete Poems of Heinrich Heine: A Modern English Version* (Boston:

The opera also had its effect on the visual arts. We have Edgar Degas (1834–1917) to thank for enabling us actually to behold part of the original stage setting of *Robert le Diable* at the Paris Opera, including the ballet dancers and the orchestra – themes that were to keep the painter busy for a number of years.[16]

The Ballet Scene from Meyerbeer's Opera Robert le Diable, by Hilaire-Germain Edgar Degas (1834–1917) (copyright and courtesy of the Victoria and Albert Museum, London)

Suhrkamp/Insel Publishers, 1982), 338; used by permission of Suhrkamp Verlag. The complete German poem may be found in, for example, *Heinrich Heine Gesammelte Gedichte* (Bonn: Lempertz, 2004), 128–30.

16. Degas painted this subject twice. The earlier, 65 cm × 55 cm, painted in 1872, is in New York's Metropolitan Museum. The second, 75 cm × 81 cm, painted in 1876, hangs in London's Victoria and Albert Museum.

Naturally, with artistic events of such magnitude taking place in Paris, the rest of the world was eager to taste these delights. Meyerbeer made a list of the cities in which *Robert le Diable* was performed during its first two years of existence: thirty-nine in France, twenty-three in German-speaking lands, and seven other countries – a total of sixty-nine different theaters.

London staged it in 1832, New York and St. Petersburg in 1834, and Calcutta in 1836. In New Orleans, two theaters performed *Robert le Diable* at the same time: one in the original French language and the other in English translation. That was in 1840. Also in the 1840s the opera's reach included Mauritius and Valparaiso. By the 1850s it had spread to Buenos Aires, Constantinople, Malta, Mexico, Oran, and hosts of other cities.

Indeed, so popular did *Robert le Diable* become that it did not escape parody. William Schwenck Gilbert (1836–1911) – later of Gilbert and Sullivan fame – wrote an amusing skit: *The Nun, the Dun and the Son of a Gun.*[17] Meanwhile, Arthur Sullivan, Gilbert's future partner in the realm of light opera, was busy editing the "Royal Edition" of opera vocal scores for the music publishing company Boosey and Co. This collection naturally included *Roberto il diavolo*, as it was called in the Italian translation by which most theaters outside of France usually performed it.[18]

From these examples it should be clear that with the appearance of *Robert le Diable*, his first creation specifically for Paris, Meyerbeer had achieved the status of international superstar. His reputation now extended far beyond the narrow world of opera. He was already forty years old, but there was still much more to flow from his pen.

---

17. W.S. Gilbert. *Robert the Devil, or The Nun, the Dun, and the Son of a Gun* (London: Phillips, 1868).
18. *Roberto il diavolo: Opera in Five Acts by Meyerbeer; With Italian Words and a New English Adaptation by John Oxenford*, ed. Arthur Sullivan and J. Pittman (London: Boosey, 1871).

Chapter 5
Superstar Status

We have seen how the opera *Robert le Diable* brought fame of extraordinary proportions to its composer. It even prompted the poet Heinrich Heine to quip that "Meyerbeer's mother was the second woman in history to see her son deified!"

Unfortunately for his health, Meyerbeer's personality was ill suited to such superstar status. He suffered from a chronic stomach complaint and was constantly beset with worries that he might not be able to live up to the esteem the public poured upon him. After *Robert le Diable*, he and his librettist Scribe set to work on a new grand opera, which was to take them five years to complete. *Les Huguenots* (The Huguenots) received its premiere at the Opéra on February 29, 1836.

With *Robert le Diable*, Meyerbeer had strengthened a pattern that was to define the future of grand opera for the remainder of his generation. Actually, the soon-to-be *de rigeur* structure of five acts with a ballet in act 3 was first introduced at the Opéra by Daniel Auber (1782–1871) in *La Muette de Portici* (The mute lady of Portici, 1828). It was subsequently followed by Meyerbeer's *Robert le Diable* (1831); another Auber work, *Gustave III* (1833); *La Juive* (The Jewess, 1835) by Fromental Halévy (1799–1862); *Les Huguenots* (1836), upon which this chapter will expand; and further five-act grand operas,

The poet Heinrich Heine (1797–1856), who wrote in praise of Meyerbeer's music but later turned against him in a most vicious manner, painted by Moritz Daniel Oppenheim, 1831 (Wikimedia Commons)

including two more by Meyerbeer that we shall encounter in subsequent chapters.

Another traditional feature of the genre was the absence of any spoken words, all recitatives having instrumental accompaniment. However, Meyerbeer added several original contributions. The first was to make the ballet into an integral part of the action rather than merely a decorative add-on for the sake of entertainment. Furthermore, Meyerbeer's characters were never all good or all bad, as they had tended to be in operas before his time. Even in shaping his heroes, Meyerbeer was strongly influenced by the indecisive hero in the Waverley novels of Sir Walter Scott (1771–1832) and the romantic poetry of George Gordon (Lord) Byron (1788–1824). For example, the eponymous hero of *Robert le Diable* is unable to decide for himself what he truly prefers – the saintliness of his dearly departed mother or the rowdy lifestyle encouraged by his devil-serving father. Tension is maintained to the very end of the opera by his inability to make this decision for himself. Ultimately, the bell strikes midnight and Robert's fate is decided *for* him – not *by* him – luckily for him, with a happy ending!

However, starting with *Les Huguenots*, happy endings are out. The subject matter of this opera is religious fanaticism, as depicted by a tragic event that occurred in the sixteenth century – the so-called St. Bartholomew's Night massacre, in which French Catholics murdered men, women, and children of the Protestant faith. Whereas *Robert le Diable* had as its subtext the simple struggle between good and evil – good being represented by the church and evil by the devil – in *Les Huguenots*, the struggle is between two opposing definitions of good: the Catholic and the Protestant. Yet again, the hero, Raoul, is torn between his love for Valentine and his duty toward his fellow Huguenots. Eventually he decides on the latter, a decision that ends in tragedy for them both.

How was *Les Huguenots* received? At the Opéra, it was the first work ever to achieve a thousand performances. From there, like its predecessor *Robert le Diable*, it rapidly spread to opera houses all over the world. And if Meyerbeer had been worried – as he had been – that *Les Huguenots* might be a come-down after the success of *Robert le Diable*, he need not have been. This is how Heine compared the two:

> *Les Huguenots* is a work of greater conviction than *Robert le Diable*, both in form and content. As I have already stated, the multitude is carried away by the theme; but the more critical observer admires the progress of his artistry, and observes the new forms it has taken. According to the express opinion of the most competent judges, all future composers of the opera will have to

study *Les Huguenots*. Meyerbeer has brought instrumentation farther than any one before him. His use of the chorus, which here speaks with the voice of individuals and has abandoned operatic tradition, is unprecedented. Since *Don Giovanni*, there certainly has been no more astonishing phenomenon in music than the fourth act of *Les Huguenots*....[1]

And one future composer of operas, the young Richard Wagner, writing in 1840, had this to say about the fourth act of *Les Huguenots*:

> Whence did the composer draw the power of developing, and through all its astonishing length, a continuous augmentation of effect which never wearies and which, after a tumultuous burst of the wildest passions, finally attains its uttermost height, the ideal ecstasy of fanaticism.[2]

Another famous composer, Hector Berlioz (1803–1869), praised *Les Huguenots* very highly on several occasions. He included a number of "immortal extracts," as he called them, in a textbook he wrote on the art of orchestration.[3] However, perhaps Berlioz's most detailed and interesting criticism of *Les Huguenots* was written in a letter to François-Antoine Habeneck (1781–1849), the conductor of the orchestra at the Paris Opéra. The occasion was a tour that Berlioz

---

1. "Meyerbeer," translated by Frederic Ewen, in *The Poetry and Prose of Heinrich Heine*, ed. Frederic Ewen (New York: Citadel Press, 1959), 625; used by permission of Kensington Books.
2. Richard Wagner, quoted by Edgar Istel in "Meyerbeer's Way to Mastership: Employment of the Modern Leading-Motive before Wagner's Birth," *The Musical Quarterly* 12 (January 1926): 72–109. An English translation by Theodore Baker is reproduced in Letellier, *Reader*, 268–94.
3. Hector Berlioz, *Grand traité d'instrumentation et d'orchestration modernes* (1843). Available in English as *A Treatise on Modern Instrumentation and Orchestration: To Which Is Appended the Chef d'orchestre by Hector Berlioz*, translated by Mary Cowden Clarke (London: Novello, 1882); available as an ebook at https://archive.org/details/treatiseonmoderno0berl.

Composer Richard Wagner (1813–1883), whose initial adoration of Meyerbeer later turned to jealous hatred, by Julius Ernst Benedikt Kietz, 1842 (Wikimedia Commons)

made of Germany where, in Berlin, he heard Meyerbeer conduct *Die Hugenotten* in German translation. This is how his critique commences:

> When it came to *Armide* and *The Huguenots*, the transformation was complete. I felt as though I were at one of those first nights in Paris when you arrive early so as to have time to glance round your forces and give your final instructions, and everyone is at his post beforehand, every mind keyed up, every face alert with a grave and lively concentration – in short, all the signs of a momentous musical event about to come to fruition.
>
> Chorus and orchestra were at full strength – 120 voices, 28 violins, double wind – and Meyerbeer in command at the first

desk. I was eager to see him conduct, especially to see him conduct his own work. He does it as a man would a job he has been doing for twenty years; he holds the orchestra in the hollow of his hand and does with it as he pleases. As for his tempos, they are the same as yours, except that the entry of the monks in the fourth act and the march at the end of the third are both a little slower. I thought the more deliberate pace took something of the life out of the monks' music, but was a clear gain in the case of the march – which, by the way, is played by the military band on the stage.

It is not possible for me to analyze the orchestral playing scene by scene. I can only say that from beginning to end I found it superb in its beauty and refinement, and incomparably lucid and precise even in the most intricate passages. The finale of the second act, for example, with its stream of scales over a series of diminished sevenths and its enharmonic modulations, was done with flawless intonation and with a clarity of detail which extended to the obscurest subsidiary part. The choir was equally remarkable. The rapid runs, the antiphonal double choruses, the entries in imitation, the sudden transitions from forte to piano and all the gradations in between – everything was punctiliously and energetically rendered, with an uncommon warmth of feeling and a sense of dramatic expression that is even rarer. The stretto in the Blessing of the Daggers was an overwhelming moment; it was some time before I recovered from it. The richness of texture in the Pre-aux-Clercs scene, with the women quarrelling, the Catholics intoning the prayer to the Virgin, and the Huguenot soldiers bawling out the Rataplan, was extraordinary, yet the ear could follow it with such ease that every strand in the composer's complex thought was continually apparent – a marvel of dramatic counterpoint realized by the finest choral singing I have heard. I do not believe Meyerbeer could find better anywhere else in Europe. I should add that the staging has been most ingeniously devised. In the Rataplan the chorus mime a kind of drum march, stepping backwards and forwards, which enlivens the scene and enhances the effect of the music.

The military band, instead of being placed, as it is in Paris, at the back of the stage – in which position the immense throng of people prevents it from following the conductor's beat – begins playing in the wings at the front of the stage to the audience's right, then proceeds across the stage, passing close to the footlights through the groups of choristers. In this way the players remain in close touch with the conductor almost to the end of the piece, and there is no discrepancy in tempo and rhythm between the two sources of sound....[4]

This part of Berlioz's letter demonstrates how thoroughly familiar he was with *Les Huguenots* by 1840–41, the period in which he wrote this letter. It contrasts with his initial review upon first exposure to the opera in 1836, in which he wrote that it contains such a wealth of subtleties that he would need to see it several times more before being able to write a truly critical review. His letter to Habeneck shows how, by the time that letter was written, he had already come to grips with those subtleties, and how highly Berlioz regarded the opera. It also gives us a valuable description of Meyerbeer's gifts as a conductor.

Like *Robert le Diable* before it, *Les Huguenots* was also immortalized in nineteenth-century literature. In the novel *The Hound of the Baskervilles* by Arthur Conan-Doyle (1859–1930), the closing lines are:

"...And now, my dear Watson, we have had some weeks of severe work, and for one evening, I think, we may turn our thoughts

---

4. Hector Berlioz, *The Memoirs of Hector Berlioz*, translated, edited, and introduced by David Cairns (London: Victor Gollancz, 1969), 324–25.

Composer Hector Berlioz (1803–1869), who regarded Meyerbeer's music most highly, particularly the opera Les Huguenots; *photograph by Pierre Petit, 1863 (Wikimedia Commons)*

into more pleasant channels. I have a box for *Les Huguenots*. Have you heard the De Reszkes? Might I trouble you then to be ready in half an hour, and we can stop at Marcini's for a little dinner on the way?"[5]

Interestingly, the "De Reszkes" were real people, and an actual performance of this Meyerbeer opera is here referred to. How so? The tenor Jean de Reszke (1850–1925) often appeared in London

---

5. Arthur Conan-Doyle, *The Hound of the Baskervilles* (1902).

in the role of Raoul, and his brother, the bass Édouard (1853–1917), sang either Marcel or Saint Bris, depending upon the occasion. However, they appeared there together in *Les Huguenots* only during the seasons 1888, 1889, 1891, and 1893.[6] Moreover, the events related in *The Hound of the Baskervilles* take place in the year 1889, as may be deduced from the discussion of Holmes and Watson over a walking stick that had been left behind by a visitor. So it would have been the 1889 performance to which Sherlock Holmes was referring – "Elementary, my dear Watson!"

Moving to French literature, Jules Verne (1828–1905), in his novel *Dr. Ox's Experiment*, devotes the entire chapter 7 to a performance of *Les Huguenots*. This lesser-known piece of Verne's oeuvre is set in the fictitious town of Quiquendone, whose citizens are so phlegmatic that they do everything in ultraslow motion. That is, until a certain Dr. Ox arrives and performs an experiment on them with oxygen gas. This speeds up their life in no small measure, as the following extracts from chapter 7 indicate:

> The first act, interpreted according to the taste of the Quiquendonians, had occupied an entire evening of the first week of the month. Another evening in the second week, prolonged by infinite andantes, had elicited for the celebrated singer a real ovation. His success had been still more marked in the third act of Meyerbeer's masterpiece. But now Fiovaranti was to appear in the fourth act, which was to be performed on this evening before an impatient public....
>
> It was customary for Quiquendonians, while awaiting the rise of the curtain, to sit silent,... But on this evening, a looker-on might have observed that... an unusual animation was apparent....

---

6. Harold Rosenthal, *Two Centuries of Opera at Covent Garden* (London: Putnam, 1958), 719–25.

The bell sounds. The fourth act begins....

The wind instruments betrayed a tendency to hasten the movements, and it was necessary to hold them back with a firm hand, for they would otherwise outstrip the stringed instruments....

Meanwhile Valentine has begun her recitative, "I am alone," etc.; but she hurries it....

Saint Bris, Never... have appeared, somewhat prematurely... composer has marked allegro pomposo on the score. The orchestra and lords proceed allegro... but not at all pomposo....

The three monks... hasten in by the door... without taking any account of the stage directions... to advance slowly....

The andante amoroso, "Thou hast said it, aye, thou lovest me," becomes a real vivace furioso....

The leader's baton is no longer anything but a broken stick on the stand. The violin strings are broken, and their necks twisted. In his fury the timbal player has burst his timbals....

The fourth act of *Les Huguenots*, which formerly lasted six hours, began, on this evening, at half past four, and ended at twelve minutes before five.

It had occupied only eighteen minutes![7]

A modern reader will notice how Verne assumes that one is so familiar with this opera that the humor of the situation will become instantly apparent. So perhaps, dear reader, if at some time you are tempted to get to know *Les Huguenots*, you may care to take up this novelette of Jules Verne and appreciate the humor as much as his contemporaries no doubt did.

Les Huguenots was also taken up by several less famous writers of the period. Thus, for example, Auguste Vitu (1823–1891) at the start of his novelette, *The Second Violin*:

---

7. Jules Verne, *Dr. Ox's Experiment* (New York: Macmillan, 1963), 40–53.

> Whilst I was staying at W—— I never missed a single performance at the opera. There was a masterpiece given every night: *The Freischütz, The Huguenots, Robert le Diable, Don Juan, The Magic Flute*, etc. All of these operas were well put on, great attention being paid to every detail, so that the whole result was everything that could be desired.
>
> I do not for a moment say that the artists were irreproachable, and there were certainly not many good soloists in the large orchestra, and yet they all seemed to understand the thing they were performing, and to observe most scrupulously, the lights and shades as the composer had meant them, and as, perhaps, only a German or an Italian orchestra ever does observe them. The baritone, for example, did not attempt to drown the tenor, nor the tenor the prima-donna, so the general effect was quite satisfactory.
>
> One evening, when *The Huguenots* was being given, I set myself to follow the development of the piece. It is a most enjoyable occupation to analyse a piece and study it note by note when you know the score so thoroughly. It always seems to me that in doing this you obtain the same kind of pleasure as when, after riding horseback through a forest, you return to explore it more thoroughly, and to gather the flowers that you had not noticed the first time.[8]

These examples demonstrate that by about 1840, *Les Huguenots* had joined *Robert le Diable* in being second to none in popularity among operagoers the world over. No wonder then that the young Richard Wagner, writing from Paris that year, felt compelled to exclaim:

---

8. Auguste Vitu, "The Second Violin," in *The Masterpiece Library of Short Stories*, vols. 5 and 6, *French and French Belgian*, ed. J.A. Hammerton (London: Educational Book Company, 1901), 561–72.

On the other hand the German more than any other possesses the power to go to another country, develop its art to its highest peak and raise it to the plane of universal validity. Handel and Gluck abundantly proved this, and in our time another German, Meyerbeer, has provided a fresh example.[9]

Like its predecessor, the influence of Meyerbeer's second grand opera permeated the other art forms too.

Postcard reproduction of a painting by Karel Nejedlý
(David Faiman collection)

For example, the more dramatic scenes from the opera were portrayed by such contemporary artists as Achille Devéria (1800–1857) and Amédée de Lemud (1816–1887), and even after Meyerbeer's death Karel Nejedlý (1873–1927) found inspiration in the bathing scene at the start of the second act.

---

9. Richard Wagner, "Über deutsches Musikwesen," *Gazette musicale*, July 26, 1840, republished as "German Music" in *Wagner Writes from Paris: Stories, Essays and Articles by the Young Composer*, ed. and trans. Robert Jacobs and Geoffrey Skelton (London: George Allen and Unwin, 1973), 50.

Chapter 6
A Brief Interlude in Berlin

In 1837, after the enormous success of *Les Huguenots* the previous year, Meyerbeer began work on two new opera librettos that Scribe had suggested: *Le Prophète* (The Prophet) and *L'Africaine* (The African woman). However, many circumstances conspired that would defer the premiere of the former for nearly a dozen years, and of the latter until a year after the composer's death.

To begin with, there were family matters to attend to. Seven-year-old Blanca was growing up, thankfully healthy, and his wife Minna presented him with two more daughters, Caecilie in 1837 and Cornelie in 1842. However, Minna's health started to decline, spurred perhaps by her inability to feel truly at home in Paris. She returned to Berlin and from there made increasingly frequent visits to health spas. On many of those occasions she was joined by her husband when his own extensive travels – to supervise performances of *Robert* and *Huguenots* – permitted.

Secondly, in Paris the Opéra once again underwent a change of management. Meyerbeer did not see eye to eye with the artistic perception of the new manager, Léon-François-Raymond Pillet (1803–1868), and most certainly not with the vocal aspirations of Pillet's mistress, mezzo Rosine Stolz (1815–1903). As it happens, Meyerbeer was not the only famous artist to find this lady's voice less than satisfactory. For example, Chopin, in a letter home to his family, dated December 21, 1845, writes:

> Since I wrote the last line, I have been to Balf's opera; it is not good at all. They sing most excellently, and I hated to hear such gifts wasted, when Meyerbeer (who sat quietly in a box, reading the libretto) has two operas quite ready: "*Le Prophète*" and "*L'Africaine*." Both are in 5 acts; but he does not want to give them to the opera without a new singer, and Mme Stolz, who governs the director, will allow no better singer than herself.[1]

In these awkward circumstances, Scribe advised Meyerbeer to complete composition of a first draft of *Le Prophète* and deposit it with an attorney, so as not to incur a fine for lateness, as had unfairly been laid upon him at the time of *Les Huguenots*. The lawyer was to have strict instructions to keep the score under lock and key until the Opéra would comply with all of the composer's artistic demands. However, it would be another six years before the manager, Pillet, was replaced, and in the meantime, Meyerbeer needed to find a more conducive venue in which to work.

With such upheaval in the Paris of *Les Huguenots*, it was something of a relief – at least initially – that Meyerbeer was able to accept the appointment in Berlin of *Generalmusikdirektor* (general music director) that was offered him by a longtime friend of the family, Friedrich Wilhelm, who had, in 1840, been crowned King Frederick William IV of Prussia.

The king commissioned two important works from Meyerbeer during this period. The first was a German-language opera, *Ein Feldlager in Schlesien* (A field camp in Silesia), which premiered on December 7, 1844. The second, in 1846, was incidental music to *Struensee*, a tragic play by Meyerbeer's late lamented brother

---

1. *Frederic Chopin: Chopin's Letters*, ed. Henryk Opienski, trans. E.L. Voynich (New York: Dover, 1988), 302.

King Frederick William IV (reigned 1840–1861), who made Meyerbeer his general music director; photographed 1847 (Wikimedia Commons)

Michael, who had died in 1833. While in the employment of the king, Meyerbeer also composed several smaller pieces for court use on festive occasions – such as choral pieces and torch dances for Prussian royal weddings. In addition, he directed productions of operas, by himself and by several other composers.

However, such work, coupled with constant intrigues by court personnel who resented the king's insertion of an outsider into a domain that they considered theirs by right, became too burdensome. So Meyerbeer asked the king to release him from all duties other than the supervision of court concerts.

This gave him the freedom to travel more and to revise *Ein Feldlager in Schlesien* in order to render it suitable for a wider audience. He felt that this opera, whose hero is Frederick the Great, was somewhat too Prussian for general distribution in its original form. Meyerbeer accordingly broadened its appeal, and in a revised version under the title *Vielka*, brought it before the Viennese public on February 18, 1847, at the Theater an der Wien. *Vielka* was an enormous success there, not least of all thanks to Jenny Lind (1820–1887), known as the "Swedish Nightingale," who performed the title role. However, *Vielka* was still a German-language opera – a form that Salieri had long ago advised him to eschew. It is therefore not surprising that Meyerbeer continued working on it, changing the language, the setting, and its German seriousness. Eventually, what had originally started as "A military field camp in Silesia" ended up being a French-language *opéra-comique* – *L'Étoile du Nord* (The North star).

We learn more about *L'Étoile du Nord* later, but Eduard Hanslick (1825–1904), the noted German music critic, writing in 1875, had this to say about *Ein Feldlager in Schlesien*:

> Perhaps indeed a part of this [namely, Hanslick's preference for the original version over its French-language metamorphosis] is to do with youthful impressions and the ineffaceable memories of Jenny Lind, but the bigger part belongs to the thought that in no other of Meyerbeer's works was the German nation so directly engaged as in this. *The Feldlager* was – the long forgotten Singspiel *Die beiden Kaliefen* notwithstanding – the only German opera of our famous compatriot. This was not simply a matter of language but rather the content and the spirit. Incomparably more concise and unpretentious than *Robert* and *Les Huguenots*, the *Feldlager* contained pieces whose dramatic power and dazzling technique positively presupposed those operas. Not less worthy than these individual pieces (partially transferred to *L'Étoile du Nord*), it seems to me is the homely, comfortable German tone that permeates the music of the *Feldlager* and which otherwise in Meyerbeer is heard only rarely and quietly. In the *Feldlager*

the master showed for the first time, and incontrovertibly, that he had this tone within his ability.²

Although Hanslick also presents some more detailed technical analysis in this lengthy essay, this particular quotation has been extracted not merely to indicate that Hanslick admired *Das Feldlager* in its own right, but also to illustrate the vein of nationalism that runs through his discussion and which was characteristic of all German music critics during Meyerbeer's lifetime. Later on, it would become clear where this phenomenon was to lead.

Meanwhile, back in Paris, Pillet had retired, and the Opéra had a new pair of managers: Henri Duponchel (1794–1868)³ and Louis-Victor Roqueplan (1804–1870), who eagerly sought out Meyerbeer in order to complete *Le Prophète*. To his immense satisfaction he was now free to pick and choose his singers at will. In particular, the availability of the famed mezzo-soprano Pauline Garcia-Viardot (1821–1910), caused him to rewrite the music in order to give the prophet's mother, Fidès, a more prominent role. This was the first time in operatic history that the leading female role would be performed by other than a soprano. If this was not innovative enough, Meyerbeer employed two novel operatic effects. This was, after all, GRAND opera. The first was to have his ballet dancers perform one of their pieces on roller skates in order to simulate dancing on ice – again, as in *Robert le Diable*, causing the ballet to be an integral part of the plot. This idea probably did not endear him to the dancers, but the audiences loved what became known as "prophet skates." The

---

2. Eduard Hanslick, "Meyerbeer – With Special Consideration of His Last Three Operas," in *Die moderne Oper: Kritiken und Studien*, ed. A. Hofmann (Berlin, 1875), trans. Robert Letellier and Richard Arsenty, reproduced in Letellier, *Reader*, 151–76.
3. Note that Henri Duponchel is sometimes erroneously referred to as Charles-Edmond Duponchel, a contemporary. See Wikipedia for more on this.

Eduard Hanslick (1825–1904), the noted German music critic, who preferred the original German Ein Feldlager in Schlesien *to the French opera comique* L'Étoile du Nord *into which Meyerbeer later incorporated some of the former's music (Wikimedia Commons)*

second innovative effect was the first use of electricity on a theatrical stage. Meyerbeer employed an arc lamp to simulate sunrise at the start of act 3, and in the process he almost blinded the audience. And by "almost blinded," the present author knows what he is talking about, because the 2014 Braunschweig production of *Le Prophète*, at which he and his wife were present, employed a similar device.

In *Robert le Diable* there was, as we have seen, an underlying setting of good versus evil, within the framework of Catholic orthodoxy. In *Les Huguenots*, Catholics are pitted against Protestants in mortal combat, each being convinced that God is on their side. In *Le Prophète*, the breakdown of organized religion becomes complete, the three Anabaptist clerics using, for their personal gain, Jean, whom they have persuaded to believe that he is a prophet.

The plot of *Le Prophète* is extremely complicated. As in *Les Huguenots*, Meyerbeer and Scribe based their story on an actual historical event, albeit again altered for dramatic purposes. The situation in question was the capture of the German town of Münster by Anabaptists led by John of Leyden. The historical John (1509–1536) was captured, tortured, and executed in a most brutal way. However, in *Le Prophète*, he merely commits suicide after realizing that he has been used for unholy ends.

In spite of the complexity of the plot, the music is extremely rich, thematically and orchestrally, and this third of Meyerbeer's grand operas quickly took its place in popularity beside the former two. In fact, so popular was the music that one number, the "Coronation March," has continued to be played until this day – albeit without most listeners knowing who its composer was. Moreover, Constant Lambert (1905–1951) created a ballet, *Les Patineurs*,[4] based on the ballet music from *Le Prophète* together with four pieces from *L'Étoile du Nord*.

Not surprisingly, *Le Prophète* made a profound impression on Meyerbeer's fellow composers. Liszt created three paraphrases for solo piano and one massive four-handed work based on the haunting Latin refrain "Ad nos, ad salutarem undam" (To us, to the life-giving spring), which is sung repeatedly by the opera's three Anabaptist characters. Actually, massive as this four-handed piano reduction is, it was itself a reduction of a work that Liszt had originally conceived and created for the organ. To this day, Liszt's "Ad nos," which he dedicated to the composer, is regarded as one of the most important pieces for that instrument and has been recorded by many of the greatest contemporary organists. But if Liszt felt unable adequately

---

4. See for example Frederick Ashton: Les Patineurs, Divertissements, Scènes de Ballet (Opus Arte OA 1064 D [one DVD]).

to reduce such a massive organ work for the two hands of a normal pianist, composer Ferruccio Busoni (1866–1924), who seemed to take great pride in out-Liszting Liszt by reworking several of the latter's most difficult works into even more difficult-to-play versions,[5] was ready to oblige.

Pianist and composer Ferruccio Busoni (1866–1924), who created a two-handed piano arrangement of Liszt's mighty organ composition "Ad nos, ad salutarem undam," based on a theme from Meyerbeer's opera Le Prophète *(George Grantham Bain collection, Library of Congress, c. 1895, no known copyright restriction)*

Naturally, the other arts were quick to follow suit. Heinrich Heine, parodying the enormous gestation period that *Le Prophète* underwent, begins a lengthy sarcastic poem with the lines:

Beeren-Meyer, Meyer-Beer!
Welch ein Lärm, was ist der Mär?
Willst du wirklich jetzt gebären
Und den Heiland uns bescheren,

---

5. Busoni reworked approximately twenty of Liszt's compositions. Perhaps the most well known is the incredibly difficult "Fantasie über Themen aus Mozarts Figaro und Don Giovanni, S.697."

> *Der verheissen, der versprochen?*
> *Kommst du wirklich in die Wochen?*
> *Des ersehnte Meisterstück*
> *Dreizehnjähriger Kolik,*
> *Kommt das Schmerzenskind am End,*
> *Das man "Jan von Leyden" nennt?*
>
> Beery Meyer, Meyer-Beer!
> What's the noise, or news, we hear?
> Will you really now give birth
> To the Saviour of the earth,
> Per your promise and your vow?
> Are you near your time by now?
> Has your travail found release
> In that longed-for masterpiece,
> "John of Leyden," the symbolic
> Child of thirteen years of colic?[6]

If one is not quite sure how to take Heine's sarcastic humor, at least Walt Whitman's praise of *Le Prophète* is not equivocal. Here is the opening of the epic poem "Proud Music of the Storm" and a few lines further on that pertain specifically to opera:

> Proud music of the storm,
> Blast that careers so free, whistling across the prairies,
> Strong hum of forest tree-tops – wind of the mountains,
> Personified dim shapes – you hidden orchestras,
>
>   …

---

6. Heinrich Heine, "Festgedicht." English translation comes from Hal Draper, *The Complete Poems of Heinrich Heine*, 789–91; used by permission of Suhrkamp Verlag. The complete German poem may be found in, for example, *Heinrich Heine Gesammelte Gedichte* (Bonn: Lempertz, 2004), 583–85.

Across the stage with pallor on her face, yet lurid passion,
Stalks Norma brandishing the dagger in her hand,

I see poor crazed Lucia's eyes' unnatural gleam,
Her hair down her back falls loose and dishevel'd.

I see where Ernani walking the bridal garden,
Amid the scent of night-roses, radiant, holding his bride by
   the hand,
Hears the infernal call, the death-pledge of the horn.
...
I hear those odes, symphonies, operas,
I hear in the *William Tell* the music of an arous'd and angry
   people,
I hear Meyerbeer's *Huguenots*, the *Prophet* or *Robert*,
Gounod's *Faust*, or Mozart's *Don Juan*.
...
Composers! Mighty maestros!
And you, sweet singers of old lands, soprani, tenori, bassi!
To you a new bard caroling in the West,
Obeisant sends his love.[7]

Just look at the company in which Whitman places Meyerbeer and all three of his grand operas: Bellini (*Norma*), Donizetti (*Lucia di Lammermoor*), Verdi (*Ernani*), Rossini (*Guillaume Tell*), Gounod (*Faust*) and Mozart (*Don Giovanni*)!

In the field of graphic art, Edward Corbould (1815–1905) was but one among several who drew inspiration from *Le Prophète*.

As mentioned at the start of this chapter, Meyerbeer and Scribe began work on *Le Prophète* and a fourth grand opera, originally named *L'Africaine*, at around the same time. However, if the gestation

---

7. Walt Whitman, "Proud Music of the Storm," in *Leaves of Grass* (Franklin Center, PA: Franklin Library, 1979), 388–93.

Act 4, scene 2 from Meyerbeer's opera Le Prophète *depicted by Edward Henry Corbould (1815–1905), presented as a gift to Queen Victoria from her husband Prince Albert. (courtesy of the Royal Collection Trust / © Her Majesty Queen Elizabeth II 2020)*

time of *Le Prophète* was long, that of *L'Africaine* turned out, for Meyerbeer, to be infinite, as it was not performed until after his death.

To begin with, he was unhappy with Scribe's original libretto. The latter was indeed set in Africa, but with the Spanish explorer Hernando de Soto (1495–1542) as hero. However, Meyerbeer caused the opera to be reset around the voyages of the Portuguese Vasco da Gama (c. 1460s–1524), India replacing Africa. In his diaries, he even referred to the planned opera by its intended new name, *Vasco de Gama*. Another reason for the delay in completing *L'Africaine/Vasco de Gama* was that, as we shall see in the next chapter, Meyerbeer turned his hand to another operatic genre: *opéra-comique* for the one Paris opera house that he had not yet conquered.

Chapter 7
Two Comic Operas

L'Étoile du Nord

Just in case you were beginning to get the impression that Meyerbeer had no sense of humor, he actually composed two *opéras-comiques*, a genre he had long admired, particularly from the pen of his younger colleague, Jacques Offenbach (1819–1880).

In Paris, this art form had its own conventions, but it was not simply a comic version of grand opera.[1] *Opéra-comique* was a more concise form; productions were in one or three acts and also contained spoken dialog.

Meyerbeer's first attempt in this new art form was itself something of a comedy in that it was a revision of a revision of a rather serious Teutonic work, which he had originally composed in celebration of King Frederick I ("the Great") of Prussia. It was Frederick the Great, who had died only five years before Meyerbeer was born, who had forged Prussia into the militarily mightiest of all the German states. The original form of what was ultimately to become Meyerbeer's first *opéra-comique* was *Ein Feldlager in Schlesien* (which premiered in Berlin, December 7, 1844). It was set in a Silesian army camp – not necessarily the most obvious location for a comedy! In fact, it was so Prussian that Meyerbeer had needed to make some serious

---

1. A useful discussion of the various genres of French opera is given in Everist, *Giacomo Meyerbeer and Music Drama*.

Composer Jacques Offenbach (1819–1880), photographed by Nadar, 1860s (restored by Adam Cuerden; Wikimedia Commons)

changes in order to present it (three years later, as *Vielka*) even in German-speaking Vienna. There, it was the amazing singer Jenny Lind who had contributed in no small measure to its success.

However, for international consumption, and in particular for Paris's Opéra-Comique, a more lighthearted plot was needed. Meyerbeer, together with his friend Scribe, reworked the plot of *Ein Feldlager*: Frederick the Great was out, and in his stead came the Russian tsar, Peter the Great. The storyline now portrayed a fictitious account of the latter's legendary wooing of – and eventual wedding with – "Catherine the Great."

Soprano Jenny Lind (1820–1887), famous for the title role in Meyerbeer's opera Vielka, *by Eduard Magnus, 1862 (Wikimedia Commons)*

L'Étoile du Nord, as the new work was titled, was not, however, simply the insertion of a new libretto into an old music score. Apart from the significant changes to the libretto, Meyerbeer composed much additional music, carrying over only those pieces from the older work that he felt were appropriate. The result, which premiered at the Opéra-Comique on February 16, 1854, was another triumph for Meyerbeer.

As one might now expect, French audiences loved it (one hundred Parisian performances within a year, and more all over the country), but, as foreshadowed by our earlier quotation from Hanslick, most German critics hated it. Within a year *L'Étoile* had

Old print of the Opéra-Comique in Paris, where L'Étoile du Nord *was premiered (David Faiman collection)*

spread to sixty cities worldwide and became particularly popular throughout the English-speaking world.

In London, *L'Étoile du Nord* was first produced at Covent Garden toward the end of the 1855 season, some eighteen months after its Paris premiere. This delay was caused by the opera having to be translated from its original French into the Italian that was de rigueur in London, and for which Meyerbeer had to compose music for the original spoken dialog. Nevertheless, by all reports it was a huge success.[2] Meyerbeer, who was present at the premiere, was called out to a thunderous ovation. He was apparently so overcome by the audience reaction that when he went backstage to congratulate the orchestra, he completely forgot his written speech and could only utter the words: "Gentlemen, the heart is so full, that the words are nowhere!"[3] Rosenthal also mentions that the press devoted twice as much space to Meyerbeer's *L'Étoile du Nord* as it had given to the London premiere of Verdi's *Il Trovatore* (The Troubadour),

---

2. *The Musical World* 42, no. 31 (July 30, 1864): 481–83.
3. Rosenthal, *Two Centuries of Opera*, 109.

The Royal Italian Opera, Covent Garden, before it burned down; site of the London premiere of Meyerbeer's opera L'Étoile du Nord (David Faiman collection)

which had taken place earlier that same season.[4] The sincerity of Meyerbeer's appreciation of the Covent Garden orchestra, and particularly its conductor, is attested to, in a different context, in a letter he wrote to the *London Musical World*, quoted here from the *New York Musical World*:

> Mr. Costa gave me so many proofs of zeal and devotedness during the rehearsals of *L'Étoile*, and conducted the orchestra with such admirable talent, that I am, in great part, indebted to him for the excellent execution of that opera. Besides, Mr. Costa so far from opposing himself to my directing the opera on the first performance, entreated me earnestly on several different occasions to do so. If, in spite of this, I did not comply, it is because the hearing of operas given at Covent Garden before mine had made me appreciate the high intelligence with which

---

4. Rosenthal, *Two Centuries of Opera*, 108.

Mr. Costa conducted all the works in question, and because I could not entrust the direction of my music to hands more skillful and conscientious.[5]

To the great disappointment of London's opera lovers at the time, *L'Étoile* was given only eight times, because the theater burned to the ground, and that was the end of all programs there until it was rebuilt.

As a result, the next London revival of Meyerbeer's first *opéra-comique* did not take place until July 1864 – after the composer's death.

Le Pardon de Ploërmel

For his second *opéra-comique*, Meyerbeer was able to give his imagination full reign. The story invoked an old Breton legend about a horde of gold that was protected by a curse that would kill the first person who touched it. His librettists, this time, were the team Jules Barbier (1825–1901) and Michel Carré (1822–1872), famous today for their collaboration with Charles Gounod (1818–1893) on *Faust*. The result of their collaboration with Meyerbeer was *Le Pardon de Ploërmel* (The Ploërmel pilgrimage), often known after the name of its heroine as *Dinorah*, which premiered at the Opéra-Comique on April 4, 1859.

Whereas *L'Étoile du Nord* has many structural affinities with popular Italian operas of that era (including several of Meyerbeer's earlier works), for example, a mad scene, *Le Pardon de Ploërmel* inverts the tradition. Instead of having an initially sane heroine become mad as a result of some traumatic event (e.g., Elvira in Bellini's *I Puritani*), Dinorah goes mad at the start of the opera, when her farmhouse is destroyed by fire, and is cured of her madness only at the opera's end. Her famous shadow song, "Ombre légère"

---

5. The *New York Musical World* 13, no. 6 (October 6, 1855): 266.

(Nimble shadow) has remained a virtuoso showpiece for sopranos ever since.

This is what the critic in the *Times* of London wrote after attending its premiere in that city:

> It has been said, we know not with what truth, that the composer of the *Huguenots, Robert, the Prophète* and *L'Étoile du Nord* was anxious to convince the world that he could dispense with that intricate and enormous machinery upon which his latest and most celebrated works have depended for adequate representation; that he could render three or four ordinary characters engaging and attractive without assistance from countless accessories; dress up a homely legend with as legitimate effect as could be elicited from the fierce contentions of masses, the shock of rival bigotries, the intrigues and conflicting interests that checker the career of Courts and influence those who move within the circle of thrones and palaces – descend, in short, from the "heroic" and "romantic" to the "pastoral," still exhibiting that musical supremacy which has won for him the foremost place among dramatic composers now living and producing. If such were really the case, the sequel has shown that M. Meyerbeer by no means over-estimated his powers; for that his new opera is a masterpiece of its kind, and his new heroine, the rustic Dinorah, worthy of a niche in the same gallery of which Alice, Valentine, Fidès, and Catherine constitute the most admirable and conspicuous features, is incontestable.[6]

It is important to note that back in 1859 the music critic of the *Times* regarded Meyerbeer as the foremost living opera composer. To place that statement in perspective, that was the same year which saw the premieres of Verdi's *Un ballo in maschera* (A masked ball) and Gounod's *Faust*. Furthermore, Berlioz and Wagner were also very

---

6. The *Times*, July 28, 1859, 9.

much alive, and their works, albeit controversial, were prominently in the public eye.

After this second stint at composing *opéra-comique*, Meyerbeer still had an unfinished grand opera in the works. We recall that he still needed to place the finishing touches upon *L'Africaine/Vasco de Gama*, upon which he had started work back in the days when *Les Huguenots* had been completed. So it was to this work that Meyerbeer now returned in all earnestness. However, *Le Pardon de Ploërmel* was to be his last completed opera. He was not only sixty-eight years old, a respectable age in those days, but his health, which had never been good, was becoming steadily worse, and fate was to rob him of the satisfaction of seeing the success of his final major creation.

Chapter 8

An Unexpected End

L'Africaine was almost complete. From his diaries it is clear that Meyerbeer had intended to name the opera *Vasco de Gama* after its hero, rather than the title Scribe had originally given it and which, owing to the change of hero and venue explained in chapter 6, was no longer appropriate. However, Meyerbeer was destined never to leave the opera in a form that he would have considered complete, because, during the final rehearsals, he suffered a fatal decline in his health. The following contemporary newspaper report recreates the circumstances of his death:

> ... The next day, Saturday 23rd April, feeling indisposed, he sent for his usual medical man, Dr. Oterbourg, who observed no alarming symptoms. Nevertheless, on the following Tuesday evening, Dr. Oterbourg considered it advisable to call in Dr. Rayer, who did not think the state of the patient worse. The only thing was the fact of the latter's suffering from extreme weakness; this, in conjunction with his great age, might render dangerous any energetic remedy, should it be necessary to have recourse to one.
>
> Despite his illness, Meyerbeer continued to busy himself with *the Africaine*....

On Sunday, although his weakness was evidently increasing, he was angry with the copyist – the only one who still had anything to do – for having failed to come.

At the first visit made by Dr. Rayer, Meyerbeer said in reply to some compliment the Doctor paid him on his works: – "You are too indulgent, but I have here," he continued, pressing his fingers against his forehead, "many ideas, and many things which I should like to carry out!" – "You will carry out both those and many others," observed the Doctor. – "Do you think so? – Well, all the better," was the reply.

On Sunday, at about noon, the obstruction in the intestines appeared to cede, but it was at the expense of the patient's general strength. Early in the morning, two of his daughters had arrived from Baden, and were able to attend him at his last moments, as were also M. Jules Beer, his nephew, and M. Brandus. As Meyerbeer had not wished his family to be rendered uneasy, Mad. Meyerbeer, not having been informed, until a late period, of her husband's illness, did not arrive until Monday, when she came accompanied by her eldest daughter, and her son-in-law, Baron Korf.

On Sunday evening, about eight o'clock, when all hope was at an end, Meyerbeer, as on the previous day, turned to the persons about his bed, and bade them farewell, saying with a smile, "I will now bid you all good night till to-morrow morning." He then turned his back, and those present pretended to leave the room. On Monday morning, about half-past five, the pulse and the breathing had become nearly imperceptible, and at twenty minutes to six, a sigh, which was the last, announced that life had fled.[1]

---

1. *The Musical World* 42, no. 21 (May 21, 1864): 325.

The article then goes on to mention:

> A few hours subsequently, Rossini, who had come from Passy, where he had heard of Meyerbeer's illness, went to the Rue Montaigne to enquire how the patient was going on. On learning unexpectedly from the porter the sad news, he was obliged to sit down, and wept freely. He embraced Mdlle. Meyerbeer, who, on being informed of his visit, had come downstairs to receive him.[2]

As to the funeral arrangements, *The Musical World* goes on to write:

> The fatal intelligence came upon Paris like a thunder-clap! A committee was immediately formed to render as solemn as possible the honours that France owed to Meyerbeer....
>
> At one o'clock precisely, the procession set out for the station of the Northern Railway, in the following order: A platoon of the 3rd battalion of the National Guard, with the sappers, drummers, and band of the battalion; the bands of the 1st Grenadiers, and of the Gendarmerie of the Imperial Guard. Next came the car drawn by six horses. The strings of the pall were held by their excellencies, Count de Goltz, Prussian Ambassador; Count Bacciochi, Superintendent of Theatres.... After the car came the members of the deceased Composer's family; the official deputations from the Lyrical Theatres, the Conservatory and the Choral Society, Teutonia....
>
> The procession passed down the Avenue des Champs Elysées, the Rue Royale, the Boulevards, the Rue Drouot, and the Rue Lafayette.... Northern railway station....
>
> At three o'clock the procession entered this station, the walls of which were hung with funeral drapery, ornamented with the

---

2. *The Musical World* 42, no. 21 (May 21, 1864): 325.

initials of the Defunct, and with cartoozes, on which were the titles of his works. At the entrance, an organ raised upon a stage, commanded the departure platform. Lastly, upon the rail itself, was erected a magnificent cenotaph, surrounded by seven lofty silver lamps....

The moment the coffin, covered with wreaths arrived, the band of the Garde de Paris performed the "Schiller-Marsch," the March from *Le Prophète*, and that from *Dinorah*.

The singers and members of the Orchestra of the Opera, performed.... Speeches were delivered.... The ceremony was over at four o'clock, and at six, a special train carried far from France the mortal remains of the great composer....³

Contemporary newspaper illustration of the final honors that Paris bestowed upon Meyerbeer's coffin at the Gare du Nord railway station (David Faiman collection)

---

3. *The Musical World* 42, no. 21 (May 21, 1864): 326.

According to the journal *France Musicale*,[4] Rossini composed a funereal homage to Meyerbeer "improvised at the moment when the convoy of that great genius, whom he had cordially loved, passed under his windows at Paris." Somewhat less poetic but more informative in this matter was the *Gazette des Étrangers*,[5] which noted that the piece in question was titled "Quelques mesures de chant funèbre à mon pauvre ami Meyerbeer 8 heures du matin – Paris 6 mai 1864" and that

> It is a chorus in four parts, the large rhythm of which is indicated simply by blows struck in equal times on muffled kettle-drums. The theme is solemn and of a melancholy character, and seems to have been suggested under the inspiration of deep emotion. The words were written by M. Emilien Paccini, co-laborer in all the vocal pieces which have recently proceeded from Rossini's pen.

The first verse is:

> *Pleure! pleure! Muse sublime.*
> *Pleure un tel fils mis au tombeau.*
> *La Gloire touche au noir abîme:*
> *un grand artiste est la victime.*
> *Pleure! Pleure! D'un jour trop beau*
> *s'éteint, s'eteint, le flambeau.*

> Weep! weep! o muse sublime.
> Weep that such a son lies entombed.
> Glory has reached its darkest abyss:
> a great artist is the victim.
> Weep! Weep! On such a fine day
> Extinguished is the light, extinguished.

---

4. Quoted in English in *The Musical World* 42, no. 29 (July 16, 1864): 457.
5. Quoted in English in *The Musical World* 42, no. 30 (July 23, 1864): 472.

The piece has been recorded by several groups, including one known as Die Singphoniker.[6]

Composer Gioachino Rossini (1792–1868), a lifelong friend of Meyerbeer, who composed a deeply moving funeral dirge upon the latter's death; photographed by Étienne Carjat, 1865 (restored by Adam Cuerden; Wikimedia Commons)

In spite of Rossini's evident grief at Meyerbeer's unexpected death, an amusing anecdote about him has come down to us illustrating his well-known biting sense of humor. Apparently, when Meyerbeer's nephew asked the famous composer his opinion about a march that he had written for his uncle's funeral, Rossini replied:

---

6. *Die Singphoniker: Singphonic Rossini* (CPO 999 200-2 [one CD]).

"Excellent, but wouldn't it have been better if you had died and your uncle had written the march?"[7]

Even Berlioz, upon hearing the news of Meyerbeer's unexpected end, expressed sadness in a letter to a friend:

> It's cold, it's raining; there's something indefinably sad and prosaic floating in the air.... Half of our little musical world (including myself) is sad; the other half is cheerful, because Meyerbeer has just died. We were to have dined together....[8]

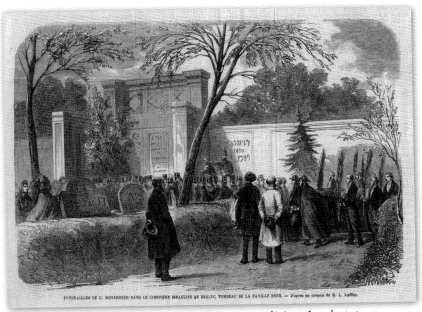

Contemporary newspaper illustration of Meyerbeer's state funeral in Berlin (David Faiman collection)

---

7. This story may be apocryphal, but according to Richard Osborne in *Rossini* (London: J.M. Dent, 1986), 119, it was one that Verdi enjoyed telling.
8. Hector Berlioz, letter to Humbert Ferrand, May 4, 1864. Quoted in English translation in *Selected Letters of Berlioz*, ed. Hugh Macdonald, trans. Roger Nichols (New York: W.W. Norton, 1997), 429.

After the lengthy ceremony at the Gare du Nord, Meyerbeer's coffin was loaded aboard the train, which wended its way slowly to Berlin accompanied by hosts of mourners from the world of arts and letters and stopping briefly at several stations along the route in order to allow others to pay their last respects. At the final stop it was unloaded and taken, ceremonially, to Berlin's Jewish cemetery in the Schoenhauserallee, where Meyerbeer was laid to rest in the family mausoleum.

In the meantime, the composer and musicologist François-Joseph Fétis (1784–1871) was charged with the task of preparing Meyerbeer's almost-complete fourth grand opera for staging. Under

From a nineteenth-century set of Liebig Meat Extract trading cards illustrating letters of the alphabet by characters from famous operas; R for unidentified Rosa; U for Uriasse from Gounod's Mireille; S for Sélika and V for Vasco de Gama, both from Meyerbeer's L'Africaine (David Faiman collection)

its original title, *l'Africaine* received its first performance at the Opéra on April 28, 1865, and, strange to say, this heavily cut version – to the extent of making nonsense of the plot – quickly joined the ranks of Meyerbeer's most-performed operas all over the world.

Fortunately, modern scholarship has restored much of the music that Fétis removed and has reconstructed a performable version that is probably closer to Meyerbeer's final intentions. At least his preferred title *Vasco de Gama* has been restored. It was first performed as such at Chemnitz, a recording of which is available as a four-CD set.[9]

---

9. *Giacomo Meyerbeer: Vasco de Gama* (CPO 777 828–2 [four CDs]).

Chapter 9

Meyerbeer's Music

Having thus far presented an outline of Meyerbeer's life, it is time to introduce his music. At present we live in a world in which a large number of lovers of serious music are unable to read a musical score. Therefore, to employ staff notation for the presentation of musical examples – as is conventional in more scholarly works than this – would defeat the purpose of the present chapter, which is to try to satisfy what by now should be some readers' curiosity to hear examples of Meyerbeer's music.

What about verbal description? The playwright George Bernard Shaw, who started his professional career as a music critic under the nom de plume Corno di Basetto, once parodied the style of one of his fellow critics, claiming that the latter might analyze "To be or not to be: that is the question" as:

> Shakespear [sic], dispensing with the customary exordium, announces his subject at once in the infinitive, in which mood it is presently repeated after a short connecting passage in which, brief as it is, we recognize the alternative and negative forms on which so much of the significance of the repetition depends. Here we reach a colon; and a pointed pository phrase, in which

the accent falls decisively on the relative pronoun, brings us to the first full stop.[1]

The verbal description that Shaw was parodying is the following analysis of part of Mozart's famous Symphony no. 40:

> The principal subject, hitherto only heard in the treble, is transferred to the bass (Ex. 28), the violins playing a new counterpoint to it instead of the original mere accompaniment figure of the first part. Then the parts are reversed, the violins taking the subject and the basses the counterpoint figure, and so on till we come to a close on the dominant of D minor, a nearly related key (commencement of Ex. 29), and then comes the passage by which we return to the first subject in its original form and key.[2]

Did that make you want to run out and buy a recording of Mozart's Fortieth? Probably not.

Fortunately, these days there are various internet sites, such as YouTube, that may be consulted for a quick taste, followed by commercial recordings, when they exist, for more detailed study. Thus, on the one hand, it is not necessary to set down staffs full of quarter notes, eighth notes, etc. On the other, nor is it necessary to quote verbose descriptions, no matter how beautiful they may be, because, ultimately, they cannot speak for the music.

This chapter will accordingly employ YouTube illustrations for a selection of what are often called "highlights" from Meyerbeer's operas. In fact, this is a misnomer, because each opera is so redolent with music that the term *highlights* is an unwarranted judgment that the rest of the opera is somehow inferior. Therefore, the following

---

1. Bernard Shaw, *Music in London, 1890–94*, vol. 2 (London: Constable, 1932), 321.
2. Shaw, *Music in London*, vol. 2, 321.

extracts – a better word – are intended to give the reader a flavor of the kind of musical creations that are waiting to be rediscovered by today's music lovers and, eventually, opera-house managers too.

Robert le Diable

Meyerbeer's first grand opera, *Robert le Diable*, is a good starting point.

Robert le Diable is an invented story around the legend of Robert of Normandy, the father of William the Conqueror, who invaded England in 1066. It involves knights in armor, a beautiful princess, magic, and the Church versus the Devil. The two principal male characters are Robert (tenor) and Bertram (bass), who is actually Robert's father, a fact unknown to the son until Bertram reveals it in the final scene. The two principal female characters are Robert's half sister Alice (soprano) and the Princess of Sicily, Isabelle (soprano), with whom Robert is in love. Bertram is in league with the Devil, to whom he must deliver Robert's soul by the end of the opera or suffer dire consequences. Throughout the opera's five acts, Bertram, in the guise of Robert's good friend, adopts various ploys for endearing his son to devilry: rowdiness, drink, promiscuity, gambling, etc. However, he ultimately fails – not because Robert chooses good over evil but, rather, owing to the son's inability to make up his own mind. Robert is literally "saved by the bell," which sounds at the end, heralding Bertram's descent to Hell – somewhat akin to the fate of Mozart's Don Giovanni.

Our first example is the soprano aria "Robert, Robert, toi que j'aime" from act 4. Isabelle, who has just awakened from a magically induced sleep, tries to persuade Robert, who loves her, that she could love him too if only he would give up his wicked lifestyle. The English translation[3] of the French text illustrates how banal the lyrics of musically beautiful operatic arias often are:

---

3. Arsenty and Letellier, *Libretti*, vol. 3, 339–41.

A nineteenth-century Liebig Meat Extract trade card depicting Robert le Diable, *act 5, scene 3: Robert torn between the call of Bertram, the devil's disciple and his newly revealed father; and that of his half-sister, Alice, representing the plea of his recently departed saintly mother (David Faiman collection)*

Isabelle: Robert, Robert, you whom I love, And who received my vow, You see my fear!... Mercy, mercy for yourself, And mercy for me! [*Robert*: No, no, no, no!]. *Isabelle*: Mercy for yourself! [*Robert*: No, no, no, no!]. *Isabelle*: Mercy for me!... What, has your heart forgotten Its sweetest promise? You once paid homage to me, Now I kneel before you!... Mercy, mercy for yourself, And mercy for me!... [*Robert*: No, no, no, no!]. *Isabelle*: Mercy for yourself! [*Robert*: No, no, no, no!]. *Isabelle*: Mercy for me!... Mercy for yourself!... Oh, my beloved, You whom I adore, You see my fear!... Ah! Mercy, mercy for yourself, And mercy for me!...

It is sung by the immortal voice of Beverly Sills.[4]

---

4. *Beverly Sills: The Great Recordings* (Deutsche Grammophon 474 947–2 GM2 [two CDs]). Extract at https://www.youtube.com/watch?v=umbOuKEgZuA.

For readers who would like to try the complete opera, a number of commercial recordings are available, all taken from live productions. Two are sets of CDs, on three disks each. The set, conducted by Renato Palumbo, on the Dynamic label,[5] captures a live, outdoor performance at Martina Franca in 2000. The other, conducted by Daniel Oren, on the Brilliant Classics label,[6] records a concert performance in Salerno in 2012. However, pride of place must go to the Royal Opera House, Covent Garden production of 2012, also conducted by Daniel Oren, released on a pair of DVDs by the Opus Arte label.[7] In spite of the Monty Pythonesque stage settings of the latter – not inappropriate for a story that involves magic and knights in armor – the performance will probably long present a benchmark against which all future productions will be judged because of the excellence of all performers. The principal roles were:

Robert (tenor):	Bryan Hymel
Bertram (bass):	John Relyea
Alice (soprano):	Marina Poplavskaya
Isabelle (soprano):	Patrizia Ciofi
Raimbaut (tenor):	Jean-François Borras
Stage director:	Laurent Pelly

Les Huguenots

Meyerbeer's second grand opera, *Les Huguenots*, is a tragic love story that is based upon an actual historical event, the St. Bartholomew's Day massacre (August 24, 1572). Whereas *Robert le Diable* has been interpreted as a human struggle between good (as represented by the Church) and evil (as personified by the Devil), *Les Huguenots* focuses on the struggle between the Catholics and the

---

5. *Meyerbeer: Robert le Diable* (Dynamic CDS 368/1–3 [three CDs]).
6. *Meyerbeer: Robert le Diable* (Brilliant Classics 94604 [three CDs]).
7. *Meyerbeer: Robert le Diable* (Opus Arte DVD OA 1106 D [two DVDs]).

newly emerged French Protestant movement (the Huguenots), each convinced that God is on their side and that the other side represents darkest evil.

There are six principal characters: a tenor, Raoul (Protestant); a baritone, Nevers (Catholic); two basses, St. Bris (Catholic) and Marcel (Protestant); two sopranos, Marguerite de Valois (Catholic) and Valentine (Catholic at the start, but becoming a Protestant convert in the final scene). There is also a minor, albeit diva, role, the page, Urbain, sung either by a soprano or a mezzo-soprano.

In act 1, Valentine breaks off her engagement to fellow Catholic Nevers, at the behest of Queen Marguerite, who fancies that she can make peace between Catholics and Protestants. To this end, she plans for Valentine, her lady-in-waiting, to marry the Protestant, Raoul.

However, in act 2, the latter rejects the match owing to a misunderstanding that has occurred in act 1.

Nevers, ever the gentleman, then steps in and marries Valentine, in act 3, as he had originally intended.

In act 4, Valentine's father, St. Bris, and his fellow Catholics plot the St. Bartholomew's Day massacre – an action that Nevers resolutely refuses to have anything to do with. In parallel, Valentine and Raoul, who overhear the plot, discover that they still love one another. However, much as Valentine pleads with Raoul to remain with her and save his life, he leaves, determined to warn his comrades.

In act 5, Valentine confronts the by-now wounded Raoul and Marcel, informing them that Nevers is dead and that she is thus free to marry Raoul. For this purpose she agrees to become a Protestant. Marcel marries them, and then the three are attacked by a group of Catholic soldiers led by St. Bris. The opera ends with father shooting daughter, who, in her dying moments, proffers him Christian forgiveness.

The extract chosen from *Les Huguenots* is the aria "Piff, paff,

A nineteenth-century Liebig Meat Extract trade card depicting Les Huguenots, *act 4, scene 3: Valentine pleading with Raoul to save himself by remaining with her (David Faiman collection)*

piff, paff!" from act 1, sung by the chocolaty bass voice of Nicolai Ghiaurov. In this aria, Marcel, an extremist Huguenot, vents his spleen on his Catholic hosts, who have goaded him into singing a song for their entertainment at the party to which his master, Raoul, has been invited, but which he has "gate crashed." The song he sings commemorates one of those rare battles in which the Huguenots succeeded in achieving victory over their Catholic opponents. The song is remarkable, among other things, for the sounds of the high-pitched piccolo and drums that accompany the bass singer. Its English translation is:

> *Marcel*: Piff, paff, piff, paff! It's over for the monasteries! Down with the monks, War against all Pharisees! War against the papists! To the sword and flame With their infernal temples, Burn 'em to the ground!... Knock them down, smash them, Crush them, run 'em through!... Piff, paff, pouff, smash them! Piff, paff, pouff, crush them! Piff paff, piff paff, piff paff!... Let

them cry, Let them die, But mercy, never!...No, no, no, never! Etc. [*The Nobles*: Ha, ha, ha, ha, ha! Listen to his tender words! Have mercy, mercy on our fears! *Tavannes*: Mercy! *Cossé*: Pity!] *Marcel*: My arm never waivered At the cries of women! A curse on those Delilahs Who corrupt men's souls! We'll destroy their hellish charms With the edge of a sword! We'll destroy their hellish charms!... Those enticing demons, drive them out, Hunt them down, run 'em through!... Piff, paff, pouff, drive them out! Piff, paff, pouff, hunt them down! Piff paff, piff paff, piff paff!... Let them cry, Let them die, But mercy, never!... No, no, no, never!... etc.[8]

Among the modern recordings, pride of place must go to the 1970 London/Decca studio recording, sporting a star-spangled cast, headed by Joan Sutherland and conducted by her husband, Richard Bonynge. It is available on a four-CD set.[9] Also highly recommended is another four-CD set on the Erato label,[10] conducted by Cyril Diederich. Both of these recordings feature the bass Nicolai Ghiaurov in the role of Marcel illustrated above. There is also a recording, on three CDs on the Dynamic label,[11] of a live performance at Martina Franca in 2002, conducted by Renato Palumbo.

Two DVD recordings of live productions are also to be found. One, in German, conducted by Stefan Soltesz, is on the Arthaus label.[12] The other, in the original French, and in a more traditional stage setting, is on the Kultur label.[13] The latter is of special interest because it was Joan Sutherland's farewell performance, at the Sydney

---

8. Arsenty and Letellier, *Libretti*, vol. 3, 421–25. Extract at https://www.youtube.com/watch?v=wGp4hFZYJgo.
9. *Meyerbeer: Les Huguenots* (Decca 430 549-2 DM4 [four CDs]).
10. *Meyerbeer: Les Huguenots* (Erato 2292-45027-2 [four CDs]).
11. *Meyerbeer: Les Huguenots* (Dynamic CDS 422/1–3 [three CDs]).
12. *Meyerbeer: Les Huguenots* (Arthaus 100156. [one DVD]).
13. *Meyerbeer: Les Huguenots* (Kultur D0029 [one DVD]).

Opera House – an opera that she chose for the occasion. Although her voice was no longer in its prime, the occasion was a deeply moving experience for all concerned, as the audience makes clear at the end. It is a wonderful film to behold. The conductor was Richard Bonynge and the cast as follows:

Marguerite (soprano):	Joan Sutherland
Valentine (soprano):	Amanda Thane
Urbain (contralto):	Suzanne Johnston
Raoul (tenor):	Anson Austin
Nevers (tenor):	John Pringle
Marcel (bass):	Clifford Grant
Saint Bris (bass):	John Wegner
Stage director:	Lotfi Mansouri

Le Prophète

Meyerbeer's third grand opera, *Le Prophète*, is also a tragic love story, of a kind. Like *Les Huguenots*, it too is set within the context of a historical event – in this case, the Anabaptist insurrection of 1534 in the city of Münster. The hero is Jean de Leyde (tenor), who is caught up in a plethora of entanglements. First, there is a conflict between his love for his fiancée, Berthe (soprano), and for his mother, Fidès (mezzo-soprano). Second, there is a struggle within himself as to whether some dreams that he has been having are mere musings, or, as three Anabaptists would have him believe, divine revelations that he has been chosen by God to be a prophet. The Anabaptists mainly appear as a trio of itinerant preachers: Jonas (tenor), Mathisen (tenor), and Zacharie (bass).

In act 1, they try to incite the peasantry to rebel against the tyranny of le Comte d'Oberthal (bass). This first insurrection fails ignominiously, but Oberthal is captivated by the beauty of Berthe, who had come, in vain, to seek his permission for her to marry Jean.

In act 2, the Anabaptists first try to persuade Jean to be their divinely appointed leader, succeeding only after Jean has been forced to give up Berthe to Oberthal in exchange for the life of his mother.

Act 3 has too many complications to explain here, but starts with a ballet scene in which the peasants skate on a frozen pond, using in-line skates, which had been newly invented in Meyerbeer's time.

Act 4 contains the pivotal coronation scene and a deeply moving confrontation between mother and son, who both, instinctively, pretend not to recognize one another in order to save Jean's life.

A nineteenth-century Liebig Meat Extract trade card depicting Le Prophète, *act 4, scene 4: the coronation of Jean de Leyde, during which he seems to effect a miraculous cure of the evidently mad woman, Fidès, who had earlier claimed to be his mother but now shams madness in order to save both of their lives (David Faiman collection)*

In the final act, the game is over. Berthe commits suicide after discovering that the charlatan prophet is her own fiancé; Jean, realizing that he has been duped by the Anabaptists, decides to blow them up and to die in the resulting conflagration; and his mother elects to die with him.

The contralto aria: "Ah, mon fils, sois béni!" from act 2 is the extract chosen from *Le Prophète,* sung here by the golden tones of Marilyn Horne. In it, Fidès blesses her son Jean for having saved her life at the price of sacrificing his fiancée, Berthe. The English translation is as follows:

> *Fides*: Ah, my son, may you be blessed! Your poor mother Was more precious to you Than your Bertha...than your love! Ah, my son! Ah, my son! Alas, you've just given up for your mother More than life, by sacrificing your happiness! Ah, my son! Ah, my son! May my prayer rise up to heaven, And may you be blessed in the Lord, My son, may you be blessed in the Lord!...John! Ah!...May you be blessed![14]

As regards modern recordings of *Le Prophète*, alas, no video productions have been issued at the time of this writing. However, there is an excellent set of three CDs, originally recorded in the studio by CBS and happily reissued by Sony,[15] conducted by Henry Lewis.

L'Africaine/Vasco de Gama

Meyerbeer's fourth and final grand opera, *L'Africaine/Vasco de Gama*, is an imagined love story involving the famous Portuguese explorer Vasco da Gama.

At the start of the opera, Inès (soprano) anxiously awaits news of her fiancé, Vasco (tenor), who is feared lost at sea. Her father, Don Diego (bass), advises her to forget Vasco and marry Don Pedro (bass). Unexpectedly, Vasco arrives, accompanied by two natives,

---

14. Arsenty and Letellier, *Libretti*, vol. 4, 283. Extract at https://www.youtube.com/watch?v=3FAAoKIve3Y.

15. *Meyerbeer: Le Prophète* (ex CBS M3K 79400; Sony 88875194782 [three CDs]).

Sélika (soprano) and Nélusko (baritone), whom he has brought back from his ill-fated voyage. He asks for money to fund a new voyage, which he claims will result in enormous wealth for Portugal. However, Le Grand Inquisiteur (bass) refuses. Vasco, accompanied by his two slaves, is sent to prison for insubordination at daring to argue with the grand inquisitor.

A nineteenth-century Liebig Meat Extract trade card depicting L'Africaine, act 1: Vasco de Gama exhibiting his two captives, Sélika and Nelusco, before the Grand Inquisitor and requesting funding for a new voyage to bring riches to Portugal and fame to himself (David Faiman collection)

In act 2, Inès obtains Vasco's release at the price of having to agree to marriage with Don Pedro – who, for good measure, steals Vasco's map of the latter's most recent voyage.

In act 3, Don Pedro having obtained funding for his own voyage, sets out and, when Vasco hears about it, he follows in hot pursuit. Vasco boards Don Pedro's ship but is quickly captured and imprisoned. Don Pedro has enlisted Nélusko as his pilot, but the latter steers the ship onto rocks as it nears its destination. Natives swarm on board and make short shrift of Don Pedro and his crew.

In act 4, Vasco finds himself alive on shore and assumes that he is the sole survivor from the ill-fated ship. Following the drinking of a potion, a love situation soon develops between him and Sélika, who, it turns out, is the queen of this land and who had fallen in love with him during their incarceration in Portugal. However, the situation is complicated by Nélusko, who, although having induced Vasco's love for Selika via the administration of the drugged potion, is himself in love with his queen. An additional complication is the unexpected appearance of Inès, who has also survived the shipwreck and the massacre of its crew.

In act 5, Sélika, seeing that her love for Vasco can never be requited, sends the two Portuguese lovers home and commits suicide by inhaling the scent of the mythical manchineel tree. Nélusko lies down beside her and joins her in death.

The tenor aria, "O paradis sorti l'onde," from the start of act 4 of *L'Africaine/Vasco de Gama*, is chosen as the final snippet from a grand opera. The aria describes Vasco's first impressions of the landscape which he has managed to reach after escaping the massacre aboard the ship on which he, his true love, and her unloved husband were sailing.

In that golden age of singing around the end of the nineteenth and start of the twentieth century, when it became possible for the first time to record musical sounds, no fewer than 204 tenors recorded this aria, many of them more than once.[16] It was, and remains, Meyerbeer's most famous aria, having been injected into the popular "three tenors" repertoire that frequently accompanies international soccer tournaments! Its English translation is as follows:

> *Vasco*: Wondrous land! Lush gardens! Radiant palace, I greet you! O paradise risen from the ocean! Your sky so blue and clear That my eyes are dazzled! You belong to me, new world,

---

16. Arsenty and Letellier, *Discography*.

I'll present you to my homeland as a gift. Ours will be these luxuriant fields, Ours this rediscovered Eden! Oh, priceless treasures, Oh, matchless wonders, hail! New world, you belong to me, Yes, you're mine, O beautiful land!...[17]

Here, it is sung, during a live performance of the opera, by Plácido Domingo.[18]

There exists a relatively modern DVD transfer[19] of a video recording from the San Francisco opera performance in 1988. The cast was as follows:

Sélika (soprano):	Shirley Verrett
Vasco de Gama (tenor):	Plácido Domingo
Inès (soprano):	Ruth Ann Swenson
Nélusko (bass):	Justino Díaz
Don Pedro (bass):	Michael Devlin
Don Diego (bass):	Philip Skinner

The conductor was Maurizio Arena, and, as in the Sydney opera production of *Les Huguenots*, the stage direction here was also by the legendary Lotfi Mansouri.

More recently, an attempt was made to reconstruct the original version, under Meyerbeer's preferred title, *Vasco de Gama*, by reinserting the many pieces that Fétis had cut out for the memorial performance a year after the composer's death. A performance of the reconstituted opera, conducted by Frank Beermann, took place at Chemnitz in 2013, a recording of which has been released on the CPO label.[20]

---

17. Arsenty and Letellier, *Libretti*, vol. 5, 713.
18. Extract available at https://www.youtube.com/watch?v=9n6ygdyO4OQ.
19. *Meyerbeer: L'Africaine* (Arthaus 100216 [one DVD]).
20. *Meyerbeer: Vasco de Gama* (CPO 777828-2 [four CDs]).

L'Étoile du Nord

Turning now to the first of Meyerbeer's two opéras-comiques, the plot of L'Étoile du Nord is not unduly complicated, by the standards of comic opera.

At the start of the first of its three acts, Peter, tsar of Russia, is masquerading as a ship's carpenter – Peter Mikhailov (bass) – in a Finnish port where he is attempting to learn the secrets of ship building. He is in love with Catherine (soprano), who is not sure at the start whether she loves him. Catherine, for her part, has a stately bearing, a quality which her late mother had advised her always to assume in her quest for a future husband. On the other hand, Peter tends to be extremely crude, particularly when drunk.

Catherine has a brother, George (tenor), who marries his Prascovia (soprano) at the end of act 1 but who promptly receives call-up papers for the army.

In act 2, Catherine has enlisted in the army, disguised as her brother, so that the latter may enjoy a fortnight's honeymoon. At the start she is reasonably serene because in the meantime she has decided that she does love Peter. However, during her two military weeks, Catherine's life becomes dangerously complicated. Peter, a captain (to Catherine's surprise), turns out to be a serious drunkard. Catherine uncovers a plot against the tsar (who she does not realize is actually Peter) but is forced to flee after Peter has ordered her execution (based upon misinformation he has received about her supposed insubordination). She nevertheless manages to get a note delivered to him, informing him of the plot, which has the effect of shocking him out of his inebriation. However, Catherine has observed the drunken Peter in the presence of two ladies of ill repute and jumped to a conclusion that induces in her a state of madness.

In act 3, all is straightened out. Peter restores Catherine's sanity by exposing her to a wooden reconstruction of her Finnish village and by playing a tune from her childhood that she has taught him on a pipe.

A nineteenth-century Liebig Meat Extract trading card in a French-language series of operatic roles by letters of the alphabet; left: O for Otello from Verdi's opera; right: P for Peter the Great (Pierre) from Meyerbeer's L'Étoile du Nord *(David Faiman collection)*

Here is Sumi Jo singing "C'est bien l'air que chaque matin," from *L'Étoile du Nord*.[21] The aria is part of the finale to the opera, in which Catherine regains her sanity at hearing Peter playing a tune on his flute that her brother used to play. Meyerbeer includes two flutes for good measure! The English translation is as follows:

---

21. Extract at https://www.youtube.com/watch?v=r9oQR-y1w9o.

Catherine: Ah, my God, don't you hear it?... That tune... I know it... who... could be playing it? Answer me! Ah!... him!... Yes, him, Peter! [*George*: It was Peter, that's for sure!] *Catherine*: That's indeed the tune that he practiced With my brother every morning: I recognize it, I think I could sing it!... [*George*: You?] *Catherine*: Me!... Do you hear? Someone's playing your tune!... La, la, la, la, la, la, la, that's the tune! Yes, that's truly it! It goes: La, la, la, la, la!... La, la, la, la, la!... La, la, la, la, la!... La, la, la, la, la!... The echo has stopped... what a silence!... Now it's your turn to play, so the echo will answer! Oh, happiness so dear to me! Do you hear? Someone's playing our tune! Just hearing it and I feel My heart beating louder; Yes, at first louder, Now softer, softer... Louder, softer, yes, softer... The echo is replying; How marvelous! Sweet illusion! Oh, dear remembrance That's going to vanish!... Slower now, More tenderly, My heart is beating, It's throbbing faster! La, la, la, la, la, la, la!... Heavenly rapture, O blissful dream! This tune so sweet, so dear to my heart Intoxicates me and fills my senses With the scent of flowers! Spring's divine melody That enchants my heart!... La, la, la, beloved tune! La, la, la, la, that's it, truly it![22]

For the complete opera, there is, at present, no DVD recording. However, a live 1996 performance of *L'Étoile du Nord* at the Wexford Festival, conducted by Wladimir Jurowski, was issued as three CDs on the Marco Polo label.[23]

Le Pardon de Ploërmel

Meyerbeer's last completed opera was also an *opéra-comique*: *Le Pardon de Ploërmel*, which is often simply called *Dinorah*, after its heroine. Unlike many Italian and French operas, which often include a so-called "mad scene" in order to allow the prima donna

---

22. Arsenty and Letellier, *Libretti*, vol. 5, 295–301.
23. *Meyerbeer: L'Étoile du Nord* (Marco Polo 8.223829–31 [three CDs]).

to show off her vocal gymnastics (e.g., Bellini's *I Puritani*), Dinorah (soprano), the heroine of *Le Pardon de Ploërmel*, goes mad during the opera's prologue and remains mad until nearly the end. Her house has been struck by lightning and burned to the ground with all her belongings. Her fiancé, Hoël (baritone), believing an ancient legend about buried treasure, decides to go after it in order to restore the fortune of his betrothed. There is one catch, however: the treasure is protected by a curse that will kill the first person who tries to take it. So, unscrupulous Hoël tries to lure a simpleton, Corentin (tenor), into being the unwitting victim. However, Corentin is not as stupid as Hoël would like to believe, and slyly fails to comply at the last moment. Dinorah then sings her famous shadow song, is caught in a storm, and falls into a raging stream from which she is saved by Hoël. His act of courage restores her sanity, and it is to be expected that one and all live happily ever after – with or without the treasure.

The most famous aria in *Le Pardon de Ploërmel* is Dinorah's so-called shadow song, "Ombre légère." In it she carries out a dialog with her own shadow, which is cast by the moon on a nearby rock.

The aria is a soprano tour de force for two reasons. First, the singer, with her back to the audience, has to arrange her voice in such a way that the coloratura echoes of the shadow are at a lower sound level than those of Dinorah, albeit still audible to audience members in the back rows of the theater. Secondly, toward the end of the aria, there is a cadenza in which she enters into a duet with a flute, the two reaching ever higher and higher notes, in such a manner that it is difficult to discern which is the human voice and which the musical instrument! The English translation is as follows:

> *Dinorah*: Ah, some light at last, and I'm no longer alone...my faithful friend has returned!...Good day!...You've come for me to teach you what you'll sing and dance at my wedding with Hoël tomorrow, haven't you?...Come now, quickly, time for your lesson! Hurry and learn how to dance and sing!...Fleet

Picture postcard reproduction of Dinorah *by Henri Pierre Picou (David Faiman collection)*

shadow Following my steps, Don't go away! No! No! No! Fairy or illusion, My dearest friend, Don't go away! No! No! No! Let's run together! I'm afraid, I tremble When you leave me all alone! Ah, don't do awat! At every dawn I see you again! Ah, stay a while, Dance to my song! Just to charm you, I'm going to smile, I'm going to sing! Come closer now! Come, answer me, Sing with me!...Listen carefully!...Ah!...Reply!...Ah!...That's right!...Ah!...Reply!...Ah!...That's right!...Fleet shadow Following my steps, etc....Do you know that Hoël loves me?...And that this very day God is going to join us Together forever? Do you know it? Do you know it?...But you've run away! Why have you left me? I'm asking you so sweetly, Why have you left me?...Night surrounds me! Alas, I'm all alone! Ah, come back, be nice! Come back! Come back! Come back!...Ah, here you are!...Here you are!...Ah, Naughty, naughty, naughty, Why did you leave me?...Fleet shadow Following my steps, etc....La, la, la, la, la, la, la!...Ah, dance with me! Ah!...[24]

Here, for example is June Anderson in a live performance.[25]

For the complete opera, there is an excellent studio-recorded CD set, conducted by James Judd on the Opera Rara label,[26] and an outstanding DVD recording of a production from Compiègne in 2002, conducted by Olivier Opdebeeck on the Cascavelle label.[27] The principal cast members of the latter are as follows:

Dinorah (soprano): Isabelle Philippe
Hoël (baritone): Armand Arapian
Corentin (tenor): Frederic Mazzotta
Stage director: Pierre Jourdan

These six French operas made Meyerbeer a legend in his own time. They so eclipsed his earlier stage works in German and Italian that one can search in vain for any trace of those operas among the 78 rpm records that were made at the beginning of the twentieth century by the singers from that golden age. The Meyerbeer discography of Arsenty and Letellier identifies 148 artists who recorded extracts from *Robert le Diable*, 590 who recorded pieces from *Les Huguenots*, 239 who left us parts of *Le Prophète*, and 547 who recorded extracts from *L'Africaine*. However, there is no indication of even a single

---

24. Arsenty and Letellier, *Libretti*, vol. 5, 409–15.
25. Extract at https://www.youtube.com/watch?v=bMI6XZ1Bf6Y&nohtml5=False.
26. Meyerbeer: Dinorah (Opera Rara ORC5 [three CDs]).
27. Meyerbeer: Dinorah, ou Le Pardon de Ploërmel (Cascavelle VELD 7000 [one DVD]).

extract from either *Margherita d'Anjou* or *Il Crociato in Egitto*, the two operas that first brought Meyerbeer worldwide fame. For readers who might be curious to listen to the way in which Meyerbeer operas sounded in recordings from the beginning of the twentieth century, appendix 1 lists the five most popular pieces from each of the four grand operas, together with their recording statistics.

Nowadays, fortunately, the situation is improving. Four of Meyerbeer's six Italian operas have been performed and recorded, as has one of his German operas. In addition, a studio recording of most of his fifth Italian opera has been issued. For a taste of these earlier Meyerbeer operas, a number of YouTube extracts are referenced in appendix 2. However, for the sake of brevity, no outline of their plots is given here. For the latter, together with an in-depth discussion of the music, the book *The Operas of Giacomo Meyerbeer* by Robert Ignatius Letellier (Associated University Presses, 2006) is strongly recommended.

For completeness, it should be mentioned that although Meyerbeer was most famous for his operas, he also composed music in a number of other genres, most notably songs with piano accompaniment and choral music. However, some orchestral and chamber pieces have also survived. Unfortunately, most of the works he composed at the start of his career, including those for piano, have not come to light and are feared lost.

Chapter 10
Meyerbeer the Man

What kind of a person was Meyerbeer? Descriptions that shed light on various aspects of his personality abound.

For example, when, in 1842, he left Paris to take up his new official position as *Generalmusikdirektor* (general music director) to King Frederick William IV, a Viennese newspaper reported:

> Meyerbeer, after many postponements, has just left Paris for Berlin.... On the eve of his departure, numbers of his admirers, both French and German, gathered in the maestro's salon, with carriage after carriage drawing up in front of the Hôtel de l'Empire in the rue Neuve St. Augustin.... Letters and messages came from all sides.... Meyerbeer had not yet returned home... [but] the salon was in the meantime filled with waiting friends, who by firelight and the flickering candles, moved about on the colorful carpets, in a hum of various languages and dialects. One observed Panofka and Konradin Kreutzer, Chopin and Carafa, Heinrich Heine and Mario, Vogt and Donizetti, Börnstein and Adam, writers, poets, composers, singers, sculptors, all waiting for the honored friend, who eventually arrived and bade a warm farewell to them all.... One cannot imagine just how much the genial and modest Meyerbeer is loved and honored here, how

everyone is intent on making the departure pleasant for him, how reluctantly they are parting with him....[1]

This modesty is also attested to in less grandiose circumstances. For example, in another newspaper article on the Meyerbeer family, one finds:

> ...When one is with Meyerbeer, one forgets that he is a wealthy man; he comes across simply as man and artist. Indeed, nothing could be more homely than a family meal at Meyerbeer's when he sits at table with his wife and three children, and has lunch like any ordinary man of the street....[2]

However, this modesty was not affected for the benefit of public relations, as attested in a letter he wrote in 1830 to a maidservant in their household, who had written to inform him of the birth of Blanca, the first of his surviving children, born July 15, 1830. Note the extremely respectful tone:

> My dear Miss Patzig,
>
> I have just received your two letters dated July 16 and 17. Please accept my heartfelt thanks for your kind reports, and please be so kind as to send me a daily bulletin on the health of mother and child over the next two weeks. I wish I could see Minna every hour of the day in these first few weeks during which every passing day brings changes in the condition of mother and infant. Therefore, your daily letters would be more than a mere godsend; they would help quell the fears and anxiety to which the human heart is subjected when an individual is separated from his loved ones and hears no news of their well-being.

---

1. English translation by Robert Letellier, *The Diaries of Giacomo Meyerbeer*, vol. 2, 67.
2. English translation by Robert Letellier, *The Diaries of Giacomo Meyerbeer*, vol. 2, 86.

Therefore, I rest assured that your kind heart will inspire you to fulfill my request punctually. Please accept in advance this expression of my utmost gratitude to you.

With the greatest of admiration,
Yours Respectfully,
Giacomo Meyerbeer[3]

Meyerbeer had, in fact, much to be anxious about, because each of his two previous children, Eugenie and Alfred, had died after only a few months of life. Indeed, so anxious was he about the arrival of his last child, Cornelie, born March 4, 1842, that in his diary he wrote:

> Tuesday 26 October [1841].... I have decided to remain in Berlin until Minna has had her confinement, and told her so (even though this is a death blow for my Parisian opera). The most difficult problem to resolve is the child, since, if he is a boy, I want him neither circumcised nor baptized.[4]

Since his two previous diary entries for that month indicate that *Robert le Diable* (221st performance – receipts 6,816 fr.) and *Les Huguenots* (128th performance – receipts 7,313 fr.) were both thriving without his personal attendance,[5] the opera whose death he foresaw due to his absence from Paris was evidently *Le Prophète*. However, as he would discover in 1849, this was groundless anxiety!

As at least three of the above quotations make clear, Meyerbeer was a family man. One of his greatest frustrations was that his professional career was eventually centered in Paris, but Minna, who

---

3. Becker and Becker, *Giacomo Meyerbeer: A Life in Letters*, 44.
4. English translation by Robert Letellier, *The Diaries of Giacomo Meyerbeer*, vol. 2, 49.
5. English translation by Robert Letellier, *The Diaries of Giacomo Meyerbeer*, vol. 2, 48.

never felt comfortable there, preferred to live in Berlin.[6] As a result, the two spent extended periods of time away from one another and had to make do with letters – which they wrote copiously. A typical example:

> My idol!
>
> I have just received your dear letter from which I see that you received my two letters from Paris and Calais. By the time you read this one, you will probably have received several from London, thereby alleviating all your anxiety.... Rest assured, my dearest, that, as lazy as I am about writing letters, this does not extend to you. My happiest moments of the day are those spent talking with you, my dearest wife. This is the way I would begin every morning, if it were not something I saved to cheer me up at noon....[7]

Meyerbeer was an enormously wealthy man, partly from birth but mostly from the success of his operas. However, not only was he unusually modest for such a person, he was also extremely generous with his wealth, and with his influence when he was able to use the latter to help a struggling artist. The two most famous examples of using his influence were for the composer Richard Wagner and the poet Heinrich Heine. In the case of Wagner, in March 1841, he wrote to August Freiherr von Lüttichau:

> Your Excellency will forgive me if I burden you with these lines.... Mr. Richard Wagner from Leipzig is a young composer who not only has enjoyed an extensive musical education but has great imagination and impressive general knowledge of literature. He is an individual whose talents deserve the support of the

---

6. The Meyerbeers' home was in Berlin at 6a Pariser Platz. When in Paris, Meyerbeer always stayed at a hotel.
7. Becker and Becker. *Giacomo Meyerbeer: A Life in Letters*, 50.

Fatherland in every respect. It is his greatest wish to perform his opera, *Rienzi*, for which he wrote both text and music, at the Royal Theater in Dresden. He has played individual excerpts for me and I found them to be very imaginative and filled with dramatic power. May this young artist be so fortunate as to enjoy Your Excellency's protection....[8]

And these were no empty words on the part of Meyerbeer, as evidenced by his diary entry of September that year:

> Friday 20 September.... In the evening I heard *Rienzi*, a grand opera in five acts by Richard Wagner. Although one is dazed by the senseless superfluity of the orchestration, it contains really beautiful, marvelous things.[9]

Having thus helped Wagner to obtain his first hearing in Dresden, Meyerbeer then turned to Berlin, in a letter dated December 9 of that year to Count Friedrich Wilhelm von Redern:

> Most esteemed Count,
> I have taken the liberty of enclosing the score and libretto (the latter is inserted after the title page) of the opera entitled *Der Fliegende Holländer* [The Flying Dutchman] by Richard Wagner.... He is a man whose talents and extremely modest circumstances make him doubly deserving of access to the great court theaters which are the official protectors of German art....[10]

Once again Meyerbeer's intervention on behalf of Wagner bore fruit. *Der fliegende Holländer* received its premiere in Berlin on January 7,

---

8. Becker and Becker, *Giacomo Meyerbeer: A Life in Letters*, 87.
9. English translation by Robert Letellier, *The Diaries of Giacomo Meyerbeer*, vol. 2, 111.
10. Becker and Becker, *Giacomo Meyerbeer: A Life in Letters*, 89.

1844, and the next day Meyerbeer held a dinner party in the young composer's honor.[11]

In the case of Heine, Meyerbeer's help was of a more complex nature. First of all, when the two artists first met, Heine was already famous, both for his poetry and also for his biting wit. It was therefore the better part of wisdom on Meyerbeer's side not to allow himself to fall foul of Heine's pen. He set three of his poems to music[12] and also provided regular monetary help for the poet. Sadly, when Meyerbeer decided that Heine no longer needed his financial help, the latter turned spiteful and started to blackmail him, threatening to publish some nasty doggerel – pieces that are not usually included in collections on the great poet's works but which have appeared, in English translation, in a volume devoted to the complete poems of Heine.[13]

At first Heine's pressure on Meyerbeer was relatively light, asking him to intervene with his uncle Carl in order to persuade the latter to renew an allowance that Carl's father had bequeathed the poet. When Meyerbeer demurred on the grounds that he did not consider it proper to interfere as an outsider in a family squabble – particularly as he had known and admired Heine's great-uncle – Heine threatened blackmail. Meyerbeer then, after much soul searching, wrote the following letter to Carl, revealing an act of generosity that he had not even mentioned to the poet:

My dearest sir,

Two different sentiments have compelled me to write this letter, and it is my hope that you will forgive me if it appears to be

---

11. Letellier, *The Diaries of Giacomo Meyerbeer*, vol. 2, 92.
12. Several recordings exist of the three Heine songs that Meyerbeer set to music: „Komm, du schönes Fischermädchen," „Die Rose, die Lilie, die Taube, die Sonne," and „Hör ich das Liedchen klingen."
13. Hal Draper, *The Complete Poems of Heinrich Heine*, 768, 772, 783, 789–91, 792, 801.

indiscreet. The first... the great respect I have for your honorable and benevolent character and for the memory of your unforgettable father. The second... on my long-standing friendship with Heinrich Heine and on the admiration I have for this great poetic genius of which our Fatherland is so proud!...

As an outsider, I would never interfere in this family matter were I not able to provide some information.... I am in this position for it was I who initiated the granting of this pension by your ever so kind father....

I can say with all certainty that your father considered Heinrich Heine's pension to be for the duration of his life.... His words were the following: "now at least you shall not have to depend on writing books to earn your keep in your later years."[14]

The warm feelings that Meyerbeer here expresses toward the poet were sincere, as demonstrated by a diary entry in 1846, upon receiving what turned out to be a false report of Heine's death:

Saturday 8 August.... I read in the papers that Heinrich Heine has died suddenly in Switzerland of apoplexy. Germany's greatest poet and my friend of 20 years dead! Peace to his ashes. He was only occasionally my friend, and when self-interest drove him to it, my enemy. Yet I do believe that he had a genuine fondness for me, as I did for him....[15]

In addition to using his influence to help deserving artists, Meyerbeer was in no way stingy with his money, as noted time and again in his diaries. He was constantly dipping into his pocket for small amounts and large. A few examples from his diary attest to this fact:

---

14. Becker and Becker, *Giacomo Meyerbeer: A Life in Letters*, 107–8.
15. English translation by Robert Letellier, *The Diaries of Giacomo Meyerbeer*, vol. 2, 165.

Wednesday 22 August [1849]. The terrible weather, with its paralyzing effect on my nerves, continues. Since Tuesday I have seen a five- or six-year-old child with the poor woman who cleans the rooms and always has the child with her. He never leaves his mother. Today this pathetic child seemed to me so exhausted, shivering with cold, that I had a cup of coffee given to him. On this occasion the poor woman told me that her husband had died, leaving her to nourish six small children from her wretched charwork. The child in question with her was dressed in what amounted to pitiful rags, and hence feels the cold terribly. I gave myself the joy of clothing him from top to toe, and made both mother and child very happy. An outlay of nine gulders (twenty-four fuss) covered this adequately.[16]

Monday 9 May [1853].... Visit from Regierungsrat Gaebler: I gave 3,000 thalers toward washing and bathing facilities for the poor.... [17]

Sunday 28 April [1861].... News from Bauernfeld in Vienna that Dr. Joseph Bacher, who has always been so friendly to me, has become mentally ill, and has been committed to an institution. Since his fortune has been ruined, Bauernfeld has asked me to make a yearly contribution of 300 thalers for three years, 900 thalers in all; I have agreed to give 600 thalers.[18]

But perhaps the most famous example of Meyerbeer's generosity was the case of Carl Maria von Weber's widow. Weber, who died in 1826, had been a close friend of Meyerbeer, since their student days

---

16. English translation by Robert Letellier, *The Diaries of Giacomo Meyerbeer*, vol. 2, 363.
17. English translation by Robert Letellier, *The Diaries of Giacomo Meyerbeer*, vol. 3, 226.
18. English translation by Robert Letellier, *The Diaries of Giacomo Meyerbeer*, vol. 4, 208.

in Darmstadt, right up until the time of his death. During that period when many Germans despised Meyerbeer for his success in Italy, it was Weber who had personally arranged for performances of his friend's Italian operas in Germany. So when Weber's widow asked Meyerbeer to complete her late husband's unfinished opera *Die drei Pintos* (The three Pintos), he could hardly refuse. However, he was an extremely busy composer in his own right, needing still in the 1820s to establish a position for himself in the extremely competitive, not to mention complicated, world of opera. By the time the 1840s arrived, Meyerbeer had still not fulfilled his promise, and *Die drei Pintos* had become nothing less than a millstone around his neck. A telling diary entry reads:

> Monday 3 January [1842].... Thereafter I went to Weber's widow to fill her in about these ideas.... The previous day she had told Madam Kaskel how sad she was that the opera was still not finished, since she had hoped to enable her son to travel on the proceeds from it. I therefore proposed to advance her the sum of 1,000 thalers for the purposes of such travel and said she could repay it to me from the receipts from the eventual staging of the opera. She turned this down, but we nonetheless still parted the best of friends....[19]

Letellier adds a note that she subsequently accepted the advance. However, matters were not that simple for the extremely conscientious Meyerbeer, as indicated in a diary entry four years later:

> Thursday 30 April [1846].... From 11 until 1 studied the sketches of the Pintos in order to reacquaint myself with them. In the evening worked on the first chorus of the Pintos. These sketches

---

19. English translation by Robert Letellier, *The Diaries of Giacomo Meyerbeer*, vol. 2, 62. The Madam Kaskel mentioned is Victoire Kaskel, for whose birthday Meyerbeer composed the song "An Victoire, am Rhein." Ibid., 61.

not only need to be scored, but also to be figured out and harmonized. In the main, Weber has written out only the vocal line, very occasionally indicated the bass, and even more occasionally hinted at an orchestral figure. What a daunting task: there is so little data, requiring the greatest conscientiousness in the handling of what does exist, especially the vocal lines, since I will on no account leave out a single note or change anything.[20]

Meyerbeer's diary entries indicate that time and time again, he offered Weber's widow a voluntary fine for lateness and begged another year's extension for this "daunting task," thus:

> Tuesday 26 May–Sunday 31 May [1846]. I kept no diary. At my wish, Minna traveled to Dresden in order to ask the widowed Kapellmeisterin Weber to grant me an extension of a year for the completion of the score of the Pintos (in other words, until April 1848), and to ask Frau von Weber to accept from me a penalty payment of 300 thalers. Minna succeeded in all of this....[21]

And:

> Thursday 14 October [1847]....In the evening I wrote a long letter to Hofrat Winkler in Dresden asking him to arrange an extension by a year (that is to May 1849) of the period stipulated for the delivery of the Pintos: I will pay Madame Weber a penalty of 300 thalers.[22]

---

20. English translation by Robert Letellier, *The Diaries of Giacomo Meyerbeer*, vol. 2, 149.
21. English translation by Robert Letellier, *The Diaries of Giacomo Meyerbeer*, vol. 2, 152.
22. English translation by Robert Letellier, *The Diaries of Giacomo Meyerbeer*, vol. 2, 250.

And:

> Friday 24 August [1849] ... Kapellmeisterin Weber has accepted my proposal to have the Pintos completed in the winter 1850–51, and to receive 400 thalers as penalty for the delay....[23]

Finally:

> Tuesday 27 January [1852]. At seven o'clock in the morning, I took the train to Dresden.... I found her unwell. Met with Max von Weber, son of Kapellmeisterin von Weber, and Karl Kaskel. I showed Herr von Weber the various contracts with his mother, where it is clear that I had already given 1,000 thalers, then for various periods of extension another 600 thalers, as well as 40 friedrichs d'or to Frau Birch-Pfeiffer for a new libretto for Weber's Pintos. In spite of these various outlays of money, Frau von Weber now wants the stipulated 2,000 thaler indemnity payment, since I have not completed the Pintos in the agreed period (which should have been the winter of 1850–51). It goes without saying that I paid the 2,000 thalers without objection.... So I am now completely finished with the unpleasant obligation of completing the Pintos....[24]

Die drei Pintos was eventually completed many years later, not by Meyerbeer, but by Gustav Mahler (1860–1911). Its rare performances are probably less a tribute to Weber, whose completed operas are giants in their own right, than a mere curiosity about Mahler, a great symphonic composer who, although famous in his lifetime as an outstanding opera *conductor*, never actually composed a work in that genre.

---

23. English translation by Robert Letellier, *The Diaries of Giacomo Meyerbeer*, vol. 2, 363.
24. English translation by Robert Letellier, *The Diaries of Giacomo Meyerbeer*, vol. 3, 145–46.

Composer Gustav Mahler (1860–1911), who completed Weber's Die drei Pintos *a generation after Meyerbeer finally gave up on the task his friend had bequeathed him; photographed by Moritz Nähr, 1907 (Wikimedia Commons)*

Of course, Meyerbeer need never have taken upon himself such a costly, not to mention soul-destroying, time-consuming, and ultimately futile task, but for him, friendship was a bond that even death could not break.

Another aspect of Meyerbeer's personality was his attitude toward religion. His diaries reveal him to have been a deeply religious person. Here is a typical start-of-year entry:

> Thursday 1 January [1852]. May God bless the beginning of the new year. May he grant my beloved family and me myself health, happiness, and prosperity. May he protect us from misfortune and illness. May he protect us from disgraceful or ignoble

intentions and conduct, or desire for them. May he preserve the prosperity with which he has blessed us; may he favor me with genial musical inspirations, and help me to put them to good use. May he grant my daughter Blanca a good, worthy husband who will be faithful to her all [her] life long. Amen, may it be so.[25]

He was a God-fearing Jew who, in fulfillment to the promise he had made his mother on the death of grandfather Liepmann Meyer Wulff (in the letter of condolence quoted in chapter 2),[26] never converted to Christianity.

There are, of course, many shades of Judaism. This was particularly true in Germany, where the Reform movement originated. As mentioned earlier, Meyerbeer's father was one of the founders of Reform Judaism and maintained a synagogue in their home. At least one Hebrew prayer setting by Meyerbeer has survived,[27] as has another synagogue prayer, in the German language.[28] This, nonorthodox religious background may have contributed to Meyerbeer's evidently tolerant attitude toward religion. This is illustrated by the deeply felt pieces of church music he wrote, both Catholic[29] and Protestant,[30] but even more unequivocally by his diary entry upon the conversion of Blanca to Catholicism:

> Saturday 5 July [1851].... In the Viennese newspaper *Der Wandrer* I read today of my daughter Blanca's change of faith. Despite the

---

25. English translation by Robert Letellier, *The Diaries of Giacomo Meyerbeer*, vol. 3, 141.
26. Becker and Becker, *Giacomo Meyerbeer: A Life in Letters*, 25–26.
27. "Uvnucho Yomar" (in Hebrew).
28. "Hallelujah" (in German).
29. E.g., "Aspiration" (in French).
30. E.g., „Klopstock Lieder" (in German). The religious pieces mentioned in this and the preceding notes are included in the highly recommended CD *Giacomo Meyerbeer: Hallelujah; The Choral Works*, sung by the Rheinische Kantorei, conductor Hermann Max (CPO 555 065–2).

fact that this took place discreetly in a small village, God grant that this news will not reach the ears of my dear, good mother who, I fear, would be very angry about it.[31]

It is telling that not only is Meyerbeer's *only* expressed fear the possibility that his mother might learn of Blanca's conversion, but this item is actually the fourth and last diary entry on that date! Far from regarding her as having died, as an Orthodox Jewish parent might have done, Meyerbeer was already calling down God's blessing upon Blanca in his New Year prayer for 1852, as we saw above.

Meyerbeer's anxiety around the time of Blanca's birth has already been mentioned. However, anxiety surrounded all aspects of his life. It may ultimately have been the cause of the chronic stomach problems from which he suffered. He worried desperately about what other people were thinking about him. His diaries frequently contain entries of the kind:

Tuesday 2 July [1850]. ... An article against me in *L'Indépendence belge* of 30 June agitated me so much that in the evening I was not able to compose. ...[32]

His operas too were an everlasting source of anxiety. As Heinrich Heine put it:

Music is Meyerbeer's conviction – and that may be the cause of all those worries and anxieties which the great master so often betrays, and which so often make us smile. One should see him at work while preparing an opera for production; he is the bane of all musicians and singers, whom he torments with endless rehearsals. He is never satisfied. A false note in the orchestra stabs

---

31. English translation by Robert Letellier, *The Diaries of Giacomo Meyerbeer*, vol. 3, 108.
32. English translation by Robert Letellier, *The Diaries of Giacomo Meyerbeer*, vol. 3, 41.

him like the point of a dagger – and he takes it as a mortal blow. The anxiety follows him even after the opera has been produced and thunderously acclaimed. He is still worried; and I believe he remains discontented until some thousands of persons who have admired his work – have died and are buried. He does not have to fear that they will turn renegades. Their souls are secured for his cause.[33]

Heine recalls Meyerbeer's anxieties back at the very start of the Parisian part of his career when *Robert le Diable* first appeared:

> Meyerbeer was at that time rightly called a worried genius. He lacked triumphant confidence in himself. He was afraid of public opinion. The least reproof dismayed him. He flattered all the caprices of his public, and shook hands zealously everywhere, as if even in music he acknowledged the sovereignty of the people, and wanted to establish his preëminence by majority vote.[34]

An unusual aspect of Meyerbeer's personality was his ability to admire the works of artists whose personal relationships with him were far from happy. Mendelssohn is perhaps the most interesting example. On the one hand Meyerbeer could write:

> Sunday 16 January [1842].... But today I received news that (if I am still able to be galvanized!) will propel me either into renewed application, or total futility. I have heard confidentially from Paris that the most dangerous and intriguing of all my enemies, M[endelssohn], who hates me mortally, has received a libretto

---

33. English translation by Frederic Ewen, *The Poetry and Prose of Heinrich Heine* (New York: Citadel Press, 1959), 625; used by permission of Kensington Books.

34. English translation by Frederic Ewen, *The Poetry and Prose of Heinrich Heine*, 623; used by permission of Kensington Books.

in five acts from Scribe and has concluded a contract with the Opéra to deliver an opera in six months.[35]

Composer Felix Mendelssohn (1809–1847), who distanced himself in every possible way from his Jewish colleague; painted by Eduard Magnus, 1833 (Wikimedia Commons)

Nevertheless, for all his disappointment at Mendelssohn's personal antipathy toward him, the music was something else. Meyerbeer was able to see beauty in it even while maintaining reservations:

> Sunday 3 October [1847]....Julius Stern gave a performance... of Mendelssohn's new oratorio Elias [Elijah]. Insofar as it is

---

35. English translation by Robert Letellier, *The Diaries of Giacomo Meyerbeer*, vol. 2, 62.

possible to pass judgment after only one hearing of such deeply thoughtful music, written with such great learning, I must say that I find it a great work, and indeed in its construction, quite excellent. But there is a falling off in thematic invention....[36]

Finally, there was a commercial aspect to Meyerbeer's character, which has frequently been overemphasized by his detractors. From his earliest youth he had been taught to understand the value of money and to use it wisely. Attention has already been drawn to his many diary entries concerning the sums he contributed to charitable causes, but he also kept careful accounts of various expenditures (travel, hotels, food, etc.) and income (from his operas). He well understood the corrupt world of the Parisian opera scene and invested money in pre-premiere banquets in order to minimize the likelihood that he would fall foul of the first-night critics. For example, one of the latter, writing in the *Evening Gazette*, said:

> How can a decent man with feeling write harshly of a man who has been pouring the choicest vintages of France and the most delicate tidbits of sea, air, forest, orchard and garden down one's throat? Try it. You will find the thing impossible....[37]

Was this bribery? Quite the reverse! It was the only way that Meyerbeer could protect himself from the blackmail of unscrupulous critics. For, as that same *Evening Gazette* critic is quoted as having written, only a few lines later, with reference to a certain P.A. Fiorentino, who wrote for *Le Moniteur*, *La France*, and *L'Entr'acte*, among others:

---

36. English translation by Robert Letellier, *The Diaries of Giacomo Meyerbeer*, vol. 2, 248.
37. Cited in Harold C. Schonberg, *The Lives of the Great Composers* (New York: W.W. Norton, 1981), 249.

> He left an estate of over $300,000, although he lived expensively.... He levied blackmail with a ferocity unknown even in this capital of blackmail.... The managers of the Italian, Lyric and Opera-Comique paid him considerable sums annually, and as for the costly presents he received there was no end of them. Meyerbeer always paid him a large pension with government punctuality![38]

In such a corrupt world, it was only natural for some of Meyerbeer's financially poorer colleagues to have been jealous of his ability to foot bills such as these!

---

38. Cited in Schonberg, *Lives of the Great Composers*, 249.

Chapter 11

The Falling Star

Meyerbeer's fame continued to last for approximately fifty years after his death. For example, the Opéra in Paris desperately needed a new superstar to continue the tradition of grand opera. So they called upon Giuseppe Verdi (1813–1901), who was most honored and happy to oblige. He had never tried to disguise the influence that Meyerbeer had had on his operatic development, having, already in 1855, during his master's lifetime, provided the Opéra with *Les Vêpres Siciliennes* (The Sicilian Vespers), an opera in five acts, and in French. So it was only natural that his new five-act *Don Carlos*, premiered in 1867, would have been his tribute to Meyerbeer.

However, dark forces were at work. For reasons that have already been hinted at and will be discussed later, not a few influential writers literally hated Meyerbeer's music. The following, by Pierre Lasserre (1867–1930), a respected French literary critic, was written during the First World War:

> Meyerbeer is dead, stone dead. *Multa renascentur,* many things will come to life again, as the poet says, and I hope that in time soon to come music will see many purely French things come to life again on the ruins of the German mania which choked

Composer Giuseppe Verdi (1813–1901), several of whose operas were heavily influenced by those of Meyerbeer; painted by Giovanni Boldini, 1886 (Wikimedia Commons)

them. Meyerbeer will not come to life again. His apologists plead the brilliance of his success. Certainly, it is an argument. But those successes belong to the worst period that French art has known.[1]

Surprisingly, in view of the war during which his book was written, Lasserre devotes two of the six chapters to Richard Wagner and,

---

1. Pierre Lasserre, *The Spirit of French Music*, trans. Denis Turner (New York: Kegan Paul, Trench, Trubner, 1921), 147.

in contrast to his negative chapter on Meyerbeer, the two Wagner chapters are extremely positive.

It didn't help that many of Lasserre's contemporaries, such as the equally prominent French music critic Camille Bellaigue (1858–1940), venerated Meyerbeer's work: Bellaigue commences a glowing essay on Meyerbeer with some sentences that already hint at those dark forces:

> The Emperor Otho, so says Heinrich Heine, once entered the tomb of Charlemagne. "The body was not lying as the dead are left in their coffins, but seated as though in life upon a throne. On his head was a golden crown, and in his hands his scepter..." As we, too, are about to enter the tomb of the illustrious dead, well may we hesitate at the threshold. Wagner is in the ascendant, and it is with a certain dread that we open the pages, perhaps somewhat neglected of late, of *Robert le Diable*, *Les Huguenots*, *Le Prophète*, and *L'Africaine*, – that first tetralogy, forsaken for another. But our fears are groundless, for in this vaulted sepulcher, Meyerbeer, too, sits enthroned. The scepter has not fallen from his hand, nor the crown from his brow, and before the grand genius, one instinctively exclaimes: "I knew not that he was so grand!"[2]

Bellaigue ends this essay thus:

> Let us, then, continue to admire Meyerbeer, endeavouring to retain in our music something of his genius, something of the solid and concrete, which reassures and confirms, and which saves us from the menacing abstraction not of realism but of reality.

---

2. Camille Bellaigue, *Portraits and Silhouettes of Musicians*, trans. Ellen Orr (New York: Dodd, Mead, 1897), 292–97.

It is telling that Bellaigue uses the word *dread* at daring to open the pages of a Meyerbeer score, and ties it to the name of Wagner.

And Wagner certainly had his "agitators," as revealed by this snippet of conversation in 1877 that took place between him and Herman Klein, a "closet" Meyerbeer lover but passionate Wagnerian:

> I ventured to remark that I thought his [Wagner's] music in the long run would suffice to accomplish the desired conversion. He turned his keen glance toward me for a moment, and paused, as though wishing to read me through. The inspection appeared to be satisfactory; for a smile suffused his features as he replied: "Yes; but here they still call it 'music of the future,' and in this land of oratorio who knows how long they will take to get rid of their prejudices, unless the agitators keep stirring them up?"[3]

That Richard Wagner became something of an idol in his later years is well documented. For example, Herman Klein also has this to say about the series of concerts in London's Royal Albert Hall, which Wagner had been invited to conduct, and on the occasion of which he had spent an evening with the composer:

> After this Wagner decided that he would conduct only one or two pieces at each concert, leaving all the rest to Richter. But would the public be satisfied? They were paying to see Wagner as well as to hear his music. The matter was discussed, and it was suggested, as a compromise, that when he was not conducting he should sit upon the platform in an arm-chair facing the audience. This course was actually adopted. At each of the six concerts comprising the festival scheme, after he had conducted the opening piece and acknowledged a magnificent reception, he

---

3. Hermann Klein, *Thirty Years of Musical Life in London, 1870–1900* (New York: Century, 1903), 72. Note that Klein later anglicized his German given name by dropping the second *n*.

sat down in his arm-chair and gazed at the assemblage before him with a sphinx-like expression of countenance that I shall never forget.

There is also circumstantial evidence that Wagner or his agitators caused theater managers to adopt an "either or" decision as regards the staging of his or Meyerbeer's operas. For example, the composer Camille Saint-Saëns (1835–1921) writes:

> Without therefore, making useless personal allusions, let us not exhibit amazement at certain judgements; here, as elsewhere, there is nothing new under the sun.... I am alluding to those, well known to be a numerous band, who flock to the banner of the mighty Richard, and beneath its shade engage in a fight that has long been inconclusive.
>
> They are not content that their god should triumph; there must even be victims sacrificed on his altars. Mendelssohn first of all.... Another victim: Meyerbeer....[4]

The mere fact that Meyerbeer's operas were becoming stigmatized was certainly a worry for theater managers and, no doubt, contributed to a decline in the frequency of their performances. But the decline was precipitous. It is nowhere better chronicled than in the annals of the prestigious New York Metropolitan Opera.[5]

When "the Met" first opened its new premises at Broadway and 39th Street on October 22, 1883, its premiere season featured nineteen operas. Among them, no fewer than three were by Meyerbeer (*Robert le Diable, Les Huguenots, Le Prophète*). That season also included three operas by Verdi (*Rigoletto, La Traviata, Il Trovatore*),

---

4. Stephen Studd, *Saint-Saëns: A Critical Biography* (Cranbury, NJ: Fairleigh Dickinson University Press, 1999), 302–4 (quoting *Outspoken Essays on Music*, trans. Fred Rothwell [London: Kegan Paul, Trench, Trubner, 1922]).
5. Irving Kolodin, *The Metropolitan Opera, 1883–1966* (New York: Alfred A. Knopf, 1968), 753–61.

two operas each by Bellini (*I Puritani* [The Puritans], *La Sonnambula* [The Sleepwalker]) and Thomas (*Hamlet, Mignon*), and one opera each by Bizet (*Carmen*), Boito (*Mefistofele*), Donizetti (*Lucia di Lammermoor*), Flotow (*Martha*), Gounod (*Faust*), Mozart (*Don Giovanni*), Ponchielli (*La Gioconda*), Rossini (*Il barbiere di Siviglia*), and Wagner (*Lohengrin*). Note that most of the featured composers were alive in 1883 (Verdi, Thomas, Boito, Flotow, Gounod, Ponchielli, and Wagner) and would, presumably, have been considered "modern."

In that first glorious season at the Met, *Robert le Diable* was given three performances and then removed from their repertoire – forever!

Next to go was *Les Huguenots*, in 1914. This was really strange, because if one studies the Metropolitan Opera's performance statistics up until that time, one finds that this favorite among all of Meyerbeer's creations ranked fifteenth in the list of that institution's most performed operas. In particular, it had enjoyed sixty-six performances during thirty-one seasons – precisely the same number as Verdi's *La Traviata*, which was not removed from the repertoire. Moreover, it ranked higher than Wagner's four operas: *Götterdämmerung* (Twilight of the Gods), sixty-one performances; *Parsifal*, fifty-one performances; *Das Rheingold*, thirty-nine performances; and *Der fliegende Holländer*, nineteen performances. And yet, *Les Huguenots* was removed in 1914 and, as of the time of this writing, it has never returned to the stage of New York's Metropolitan Opera.

In 1927, *Le Prophète* had its final New York staging after fifty-six performances (except for a brief revival, half a century later). At that time it ranked twenty-sixth among the Met's most performed operas: still higher than Wagner's *Das Rheingold* (which, meanwhile, had reached fifty performances) and *Der fliegende Holländer* (which had enjoyed no further performances than it had when *Les Huguenots* was removed).

The last of Meyerbeer's grand operas to disappear from the Met's stage was *L'Africaine*, which received its final production there during the 1933 season, after a total of fifty-five performances. At that time, *L'Africaine* ranked twenty-ninth among the house's most performed operas: only one performance fewer than Wagner's *Das Rheingold*, but still comfortably higher than his *Der fliegende Holländer* (twenty-eight performances).

Of Meyerbeer's remaining operas, *Dinorah* was last seen at the Met in the 1924 season; *L'Étoile du Nord* and the early Italian operas were never staged there.

Of course, the frequency with which an opera is put on does not

The New York Metropolitan Opera, which stopped producing Meyerbeer operas early in the twentieth century; photographed 1905 (Wikimedia Commons)

necessarily represent the taste of the opera-loving public. Theater managers are naturally mainly concerned with filling seats, particularly for expensive productions such as were usually lavished upon Meyerbeer's operas. Thus, public opinion does matter to them. However, they are only too painfully aware of the effect that critics can have on the public. Take, for example, the following start to a review of *Les Huguenots* that took place at the Met on December 18, 1891. It is by the *New York Tribune* music critic, Henry Krehbiel:

> The announcement of "Les Huguenots" for the third night of the Italian season brought out an audience larger and more brilliant than either of the two that had previously gathered to hear Mr. Abbey's company....[6]

As it happened, the first two nights of that season had staged Gounod's *Roméo et Juliette* and Verdi's *Il Trovatore*, with star casts. So the New York public clearly knew what they liked. Who knows: perhaps Gounod and Verdi were too modern for their tastes, and Mr. Krehbiel was, thoughtfully, not to claim that he knew better.

However, only three years later, W.J. Henderson of the *New York Times* felt the need to demonstrate that he did know better! Opening his review of one of the Met's famous "nights of the seven stars" performances (December 26, 1894) of this same Meyerbeer opera, Henderson had this to opine:

> It is a peculiar fact that one of the noblest, and one of the hollowest of all operas are always selected by opera managers for performance by what may be called display casts. The first of these operas is Mozart's "Don Giovanni" and the latter is Meyerbeer's "Les Huguenots." The former cannot be acceptably performed without a great cast; the latter is absolutely intolerable unless

---

6. William H. Seltsam, *Metropolitan Opera Annals* (New York: H.W. Wilson, 1947), 51.

it is so performed. Such a cast as that of last night, for hearing which the holders of orchestra chairs were asked to pay $7 each, invited recollection of former times. Last night's performance was indeed brilliant....[7]

One wonders how such negative feelings could have survived after hearing, in a performance that he admitted to have been "brilliant," the seven stars:

Lillian Nordica (1857–1914) as *Valentine*
Sofia Scalchi (1850–1922) as *Urbain*
Nellie Melba (1861–1931) as *Marguerite*
Jean de Reszke (1850–1925) as *Raoul*
Édouard de Reszke (1853–1917) as *Marcel*
Pol Plançon (1851–1914) as *St. Bris*
Victor Maurel (1848–1923) as *Nevers*

By contrast, that same critic had waxed ecstatic at a Met performance of Wagner's *Tristan und Isolda* three years earlier.[8] However, by 1894, he had decided that *Les Huguenots* was empty of whatever it takes to fill a "hollow" opera. But note the negative message that Mr. Henderson was sending both to opera lovers and to theater managers!

We might well laugh at the pomposity with which music critics often allow themselves to write – were it not for the deadly effect their words can have. Thus, for all practical purposes, at the Metropolitan Opera House, Meyerbeer's operas died in 1932. An absolutely unique situation: no other composer – and certainly none as popular as Meyerbeer – ever suffered such a reversal of fortune. And this reversal occurred, more or less simultaneously, all over the world.

---

7. Seltsam, *Metropolitan Opera Annals*, 69.
8. Seltsam, *Metropolitan Opera Annals*, 44–45.

Attention has been drawn to the New York Metropolitan Opera House because the history of its performances has been documented in a manner that renders the compilation of statistics a relatively simple task. However, the trend, as noted, was similar among opera houses throughout the entire Western world. Namely, Meyerbeer was standard repertoire until about the start of the First World War, after which his operas all but disappeared for the rest of that century.

Did this phenomenon represent simply a change in taste on the part of the opera-loving public? If so, what aspect of taste, and should it not also have affected other composers too?

Perhaps the French language? No – *Carmen* and *Faust* have continued to fill opera houses to the present time, and in any case, in those days most opera houses were performing Meyerbeer in Italian translation.

Perhaps their great length? No – many of Wagner's operas are at least as long (e.g., *Götterdämmerung* and *Parsifal*).

Perhaps the difficult coloratura singing demanded of the performers? No – Bellini's *Norma*, Donizetti's *Lucia di Lammermoor* and Rossini's *Il barbiere di Siviglia* have all remained in the repertoire.

Perhaps the enormous expense required to hire seven (in the case of *Les Huguenots*) divas? No. Such lavish budgets were not available for most of the nonetheless enormously popular nineteenth-century performances in opera houses across the world. Good singers, even with minimalistic staging, as a number of recent revivals have adequately demonstrated, are able to produce fine performances of Meyerbeer's operas.

There would appear, therefore, to be only one possible explanation, which was stated more or less explicitly by Lasserre and by Henderson: namely, that Meyerbeer's operas are, in fact, trash, and that the entire musical world had been hypnotized into thinking that they were great art until one man, Richard Wagner, came along and awakened it from its stupor.

Wagner's personal contribution to the dearth of Meyerbeer performances (which continues to this day) will be examined in chapter 13, after first discussing the background setting in which Wagner was able to precipitate such an upheaval.

Chapter 12

Meyerbeer and Anti-Semitism

Meyerbeer suffered the stings of anti-Semitism (for which he used the Yiddish term *rishus* [which he spelled in French style, *richesse*], meaning "evil") all his life. Several of his diary entries, as well as letters to fellow Jews, such as the poet Heinrich Heine, and his own family, indicate this. For example, one of his earliest diary entries to have survived is dated Wednesday, April 22, 1812. It includes the following remark from the twenty-one-year-old, still-unknown, composer:

> At midday I had lunch at the table d'hôte. Some young women there wounded me to the depths of my soul, spoiling my mood and cheerfulness for the rest of the day. When will I learn to accept peacefully what I have so long known to be inevitable?[1]

Even six months before the death of the now world-renowned composer, his diary entry for Friday, November 13, 1863, includes:

---

1. English translation by Robert Letellier, *The Diaries of Giacomo Meyerbeer*, vol. 1, 261.

Burguis has sent me the review of the book *Allgemeine Gesichte der Musik in übersichtlicher Vorstellung* by Dr. Schlüter, in which Halévy and I as composers are attacked in the most shameless way, particularly because we are Jews.[2]

In order to examine the possibility that anti-Semitism may have been a significant cause of the subsequent neglect of Meyerbeer's music, we must first discuss what we understand by the term *anti-Semitism*. For as one wag once wrote: "An anti-Semite is anyone who dislikes Jews more than necessary." This statement although made, no doubt, in jest, contains an underlying truth: namely, that in any society there is always a background level of prejudice that most people are unaware of, which must be taken into account before we judge whether a statement or action can truly be construed as racist or anti-Semitic.

For example, not so long ago, black-faced ragdolls, known as golliwogs, were common children's toys throughout the English-speaking world. One well-known marmalade manufacturer even employed such a symbol as its company logo. At that time, no white-skinned person would have imagined that such an image could possibly cause offense to anyone.

Furthermore, the fourth edition of the *Concise Oxford Dictionary*, which was widely used during the 1950s, defines "Jew" as both a noun and a transitive verb; the latter meaning "cheat, overreach." Even some of the definitions of the noun given in that edition are equally offensive. On the other hand, the tenth edition of that dictionary, published in 1999, has removed the verb usage and cleaned away all traces of offense from their definition of the noun. Interestingly, golliwog is still in the tenth edition. However, unlike that in the fourth, the new definition of "wog" now warns the reader that it is offensive.

---

2. English translation by Robert Letellier, *The Diaries of Giacomo Meyerbeer*, vol. 4, 322.

An early twentieth-century stuffed "golliwog" toy (courtesy of Karen Arnold)

We thus see how successive editions of this famous dictionary can be used to gauge the evolving background level of racial prejudice in England at various times in recent history.

With these examples in mind, let us return to Europe of the nineteenth century. A collection of stories first published at that time, which has been translated into possibly all languages on Earth, is the famous fairy tale book of the Brothers Grimm. What child has not heard of *Snow White and the Seven Dwarfs; Cinderella; Little Red Riding-Hood*; and many, many, others? However, the *complete* collection of *Grimms' Fairy Tales* also contains a story entitled *The Jew among Thorns*. One English-language edition contains the following apologia from the publishers:

> The publishers have included this story because it is a literal rendering of the Grimms' work, and is of literary and historical interest. The stereotyping that it expresses is both obvious and obnoxious, and modern readers will draw their own conclusions.[3]

---

3. The Brothers Grimm, *The Complete Fairy Tales* (Ware, Herts., UK: Wordsworth Edition, 2009), 528–32.

Nineteenth-century readers, however, would probably not have found *The Jew among Thorns* to be any more obnoxious than *Cinderella* (the latter having a clear sexist slant that modern-day feminists might well find offensive). We shall return to *The Jew among Thorns* in the next chapter.

What about major nineteenth-century composers? Beethoven, in a letter dated December 15, 1800, offers a list of works to the publisher Hofmeister in Leipzig. He concludes the letter with the following words:

> In your answer you can yourself fix the prices, and as you are neither an Italian nor a Jew, nor am I either, we shall no doubt quickly agree.[4]

Does such a sentence imply that Beethoven was an anti-Semite? By modern standards, perhaps. But by the norms of his time, he was simply expressing a commonly held prejudiced generalization about Italians and Jews in business dealings.

Frédéric Chopin provides another example. In a letter dated March 13, 1839, to his friend Juljan Fontana, we find the following sentences:

> Many thanks, my Life, for your running about. I did not expect that Pleyel would Jew me; but, if so, please give him this letter. I think he won't cause you any trouble about the Ballade and the Polonaise. But, in the opposite event, get 500 for the ballade from Probst, and then take it to Schlesinger. If I have to deal with Jews, let it at least be Orthodox ones. Probst may swindle me even worse, for he's a sparrow whose tail you can't salt. Schlesinger has always cheated me; but he has made a lot out of me, and won't

---

4. Ludwig van Beethoven, *Beethoven's Letters*, trans. Lady Wallace (London: Longmans, Green, 1866), 36–37.

THE DELIBERATELY FORGOTTEN COMPOSER

Composer Ludwig van Beethoven (1770–1827), under whose baton Meyerbeer played the timpani in the Seventh Symphony; portrait by Joseph Karl Stieler, 1820 (Wikimedia Commons)

want to refuse another profit; only be polite to him, because the Jew likes to pass for somebody.[5]

From this letter and those in the sequence that follows, one may infer that Pleyel and Probst are not Jews, that Chopin himself is quite a "businessman" (get 500 for the ballade from Probst, and then take it to Schlesinger), and that he prefers to deal with the Jew, Schlesinger. All in all, the term *Jew*, both as a verb and as a noun, although used by Chopin in a derogatory sense, was evidently a part of the business parlance of the time, which would require no

---

5. Frédéric Chopin, *Chopin's Letters*, trans. E.L. Voynich (New York: Dover, 1988), 193–94.

explanations to Fontana. On the other hand, as we have already seen, Chopin had nothing but praise to heap on Meyerbeer (whose religion he never referred to), even basing one of his own chamber works on themes from *Robert le Diable*.[6] So, any "anti-Semitism" that Chopin may have expressed or even felt was probably no deeper than the common prejudice of his era. In fact, Meyerbeer even took an important part, as a pallbearer, at Chopin's funeral. So it is unlikely that he took the latter's anti-Semitism too seriously.

What about Robert Schumann? With Schumann, there is evidence that antipathy to Jews ran deeper than mere prejudices about business dealings with them. He and his wife Clara kept a marriage diary in which they wrote messages to one another and entered their feelings about various matters. Here is an example from 1840:

> Clara told me that I seemed different toward Mendelssohn; surely not toward him as an artist – you know that – for years I have contributed so much to promoting him, more than almost anyone else. In the meantime – let's not neglect ourselves too much. Jews remain Jews; first they take a seat ten times for themselves, then comes the Christians' turn. The stones we have helped gather for their Temple of Glory they occasionally throw at us. Therefore do not do too much [for them] is my opinion.[7]

To which Clara responded:

> First I must tell you, my dear husband, that I agree with you completely in regard to the above statement, and that I have sometimes, silently, had similar thoughts, but out of great

---

6. Frédéric Chopin and Auguste Franchomme, *Grand duo concertant pour piano et violoncelle sur des thèmes de Robert le Diable* in E Major.
7. Robert Schumann and Clara Schumann, *The Marriage Diaries of Robert and Clara Schumann*, trans. Peter Ostwald (London: Robson Books, 1994), 31.

> admiration for Mendelssohn's art have again and again adopted the old excessive attentiveness toward him. I will take your advice and not degrade myself too much before him, as I have done so often.[8]

The anti-Semitic sentiments expressed here by both musicians would seem to be a degree or two stronger than those expressed by Beethoven and Chopin – particularly since Mendelssohn was an avowed Christian. However, in the case of Schumann, it has been claimed[9] they may have been brought on by slight pangs of jealousy. He admired Mendelssohn's musicianship enormously. However, the latter's promotion of Clara's pianistic career, which included several joint concerts, may have given her husband the feeling that he was being left on the sidelines.

Be that as it may, both artists clearly admired Mendelssohn's musical genius and never said or did anything to try to disparage it. This was not the case with their attitude to Meyerbeer. In their marriage diary, Clara makes the following comment about the husband of one of her aquaintances:

> An argument with her husband made me somewhat hot-blooded – namely, he asserted that Meyerbeer is vastly superior to Weber. One should really always maintain silence toward a lay person, but my zeal won't easily let me swallow such a stupid opinion.[10]

This, of course, is merely an opinion about the quality of Meyerbeer's music, not an obviously anti-Semitic statement. However, it was a comment made to her husband, whose over-emotional attitude to Meyerbeer was obviously well known to her. This attitude is evident

---

8. Schumann and Schumann, *Marriage Diaries*, 32.
9. Peter F. Ostwald, *Schumann: Music and Madness* (London: Victor Gollancz, 1986), 118.
10. Schumann and Schumann, *Marriage Diaries*, 55.

Robert (1810–1856) and Clara (1819–1896) Schumann, a composer/pianist couple whose anti-Semitism fueled each other's hatred of Meyerbeer; lithograph by Eduard Kaiser, 1847 (Wikimedia Commons)

in a scathing review he had written of *Les Huguenots*. Writing in 1837, Schumann becomes almost hysterical in his condemnation of the opera:

> Still elated by Schröder-Devrient's lofty performance of *Fidelio*, I went to hear *Les Huguenots* for the first time. Who does not gladly hope? Had not Ries himself written that some passages in *Les Huguenots* might be placed beside some of Beethoven's, etc.? And what said others, what said I? I agreed entirely with Florestan who, shaking his fist at the opera house, let fall these

words: "In *Il Crociato* I still counted Meyerbeer among the musicians; in *Robert le Diable* I began to waver; beginning with *Les Huguenots* I unhesitatingly rank him among the performers in Franconi's circus." I cannot express the aversion which the whole work inspired in us; we turned away from it – we were weary and exhausted with anger. After repeated hearings I found much that was excusable, that impressed me more favorably. My final judgment nonetheless remained the same as heretofore, and I must shout incessantly to those who even remotely compare *Les Huguenots* with *Fidelio*, or any similar work, that they understand nothing of the matter – nothing, nothing! I certainly shall not attempt a conversion – one would not know where to begin and where to end.[11]

As an aside, Florestan and Eusebius were two imaginary characters whom Schumann invented for use in his music criticisms, Florestan generally being the more critical of the two.

As for Schumann's infamous "Franconi's circus" description, it is entirely possible that it was brought about by the way the part of Valentine was enacted by the famous soprano diva Wilhelmine Schröder-Devrient (1804–1860) in this German-language performance. How come? As it happens, we have Berlioz's review of what was possibly the very same production. It was in a continuation to the letter quoted earlier in this book:

> ...I had no bias nor predisposition for or against Madame Devrient. I remembered only that I thought her admirable in Beethoven's *Fidelio* in Paris many years ago, whereas in Dresden recently I had noticed some very bad habits in her singing and a tendency to overemphasis and affectation in her acting. In *Les Huguenots* I found these defects all the more striking because

---

11. Robert Schumann, *On Music and Musicians*, ed. Konrad Wolff, trans. Paul Rosenfeld (New York: Pantheon Books, 1946), 194–97.

the dramatic situations are more vivid and the music correspondingly grander and truer. I therefore criticized the singer and the actress, on the following grounds. In the conjuration scene Valentine, though horrified when her father reveals to Nevers and his friends his plan to massacre the Huguenots, is careful not to show her feelings, Saint-Bris being hardly the man to tolerate such an attitude in his daughter. Thus her sudden involuntary gesture towards her husband, Nevers, the instant he breaks his sword and refuses to have anything to do with the conspiracy, is a fine dramatic stroke which depends for its effect on the timid woman having until then suffered her agonies of spirit in silence. Madame Devrient, instead of concealing her agitation and remaining to all appearances impassive, as sense clearly requires in such a scene, seizes hold of Nevers and drags him to the back of the stage where, pacing masterfully at his side, she appears to be dictating his best plan of action and instructing him as to how he shall answer Saint-Bris. Consequently Nevers' exclamation, "I count soldiers among my proud ancestors but never a murderer," loses all its merit as an impulse of bold opposition; the gesture ceases to be spontaneous, Nevers having the air of a submissive husband dutifully repeating what his wife has told him. When Saint-Bris delivers the famous theme "A cette cause sainte," Madame Devrient actually forgets herself so far as to spring into his arms (although Saint-Bris is supposed to be still unaware of his daughter's feelings) and importune him with a dumb show of such vehemence that Boeticher, visibly taken aback by this unseasonable outburst, the first time it occurred, and hard put to preserve freedom of wind and limb, executed frantic movements with his head and right arm, as though to say, "For God's sake leave me be, woman, and allow me to sing my role to the end." The incident demonstrates the extent to which Madame Devrient has succumbed to the demon of personality; she would consider herself to have failed if she did not monopolize the attention of the house, rightly or wrongly and by whatever piece of stage business, in every scene she appears in. Her whole manner suggests that she sees herself as the focus of the drama, the only character with whom the audience need concern itself. "What? Listening to that fellow? Admiring the composer? Interested in that chorus? How can you be so misguided? Look over here, this is what you should be attending to. I am the libretto, I am the poetry, I am the music. The one object of interest this evening is me. The sole reason for your coming to the theatre is me!" During the tremendous duet which follows this great scene, while Raoul abandons himself to the frenzy of his despair, Madame Devrient rests her hands decorously on a settee and inclines her head to the left so as to let her fine blond hair fall free. She sings a phrase or two and then, while Raoul replies, changes her pose, to allow the audience to admire the soft glow and play of her ringlets from a different angle. I take leave to question whether it is with such considerations of coquettish personal vanity that Valentine's mind is occupied at this particular moment.[12]

According to Berlioz's review, the famous German soprano indeed acted the part somewhat like a circus clown. However, the French composer was able to distinguish her poor acting from the overall musical excellence of the performance, which he analyzes in great detail, as we saw in chapter 5.

Returning to Schumann's essay, he now goes on to pass moral judgment upon the structure of *Les Huguenots*:

> ... What can be the opera's next step after *Les Huguenots* save the execution of criminals and the exhibition of gay harlots? Reflect on the whole, and what does it amount to? In the first act we have a masculine orgy, including – oh, how clever! – only one

---

12. Berlioz, *Memoirs*, 325–26.

woman, but a veiled one! In the second a revel of bathing women, and, among them – as carrion for the Parisians – a man, he with bandaged eyes. In the third act the lewd tendency is mixed with the sacred; slaughter is prepared in the fourth, and in the fifth it is carried out in a church. Debauchery, murder, and prayer; this, and nothing else, makes *Les Huguenots*. It would be vain to seek for one pure, lasting idea, one spark of Christian feeling in it. Meyerbeer nails the heart to the skin and cries: "Look! there it is, for all to see!" Everything is artificial, everything pretense and hypocrisy. And then these heroes and heroines – two alone excepted: Marcel and St. Bris, who do not sink so low as the rest. There is Nevers, the perfect French debauchee who loves Valentine, gives her up, and then takes her for his wife; Valentine herself, who loves Raoul, marries Nevers, swears she loves him, and then in the end plights troth to Raoul; Raoul, who loves Valentine, rejects her, falls in love with the Queen, and finally takes Valentine to wife; finally the Queen, the queen of all these puppets! And people are pleased with this because it is gratifying to the eye and comes from Paris! And you respectable German girls, is it possible you do not hide your eyes? And the archfox of all composers rubs his hands with joy!

Were Schumann comparing Meyerbeer's *Les Huguenots* with Beethoven's *Fidelio*, according to the Protestant moral grounds he professes to espouse, he might have a point. After all, Beethoven's opera features a woman who leaves no stone unturned to locate and ultimately release her imprisoned husband. The opera contains, possibly uniquely for the genre, absolutely no sexual dilly-dallying. Consequently, one wonders how Schumann might have reacted to the blatantly "immoral" (by Schumann's standards!) sexuality of Mozart masterpieces such as *Le Nozze di Figaro, Cosi fan tutte, Don Giovanni*. But we need not wonder, because we have Schumann's reaction to Chopin's variations for piano on the aria "La ci darem la mano" from *Don Giovanni*, in which it will be recalled that the don is here attempting to seduce Zerlina on the eve of her wedding to Masetto:

> ...Don Juan, Zerlina, Leporello, and Masetto are the *dramatis personae*; Zerlina's answer in the theme has a sufficiently amorous character; the first variation might be called distinguished and coquettish – the Spanish grandee flirting amiably with the peasant girl. The flirtation develops in the most natural way in the second, which is much more intimate, comic, and quarrelsome, as though two lovers were laughingly chasing each other.... It is both mischievous and suitable that Leporello should listen behind the hedge, chuckling and jesting....[13]

By the moral standards that Schumann is preaching to "respectable German girls," *Les Huguenots* is as chaste as *Fidelio* if we compare these operas with *Don Giovanni*! So, wherein lies the difference? The Protestant Schumann's first implied hint is that whereas Beethoven and Mozart were both Catholics, "the archfox of all composers [who] rubs his hands with joy" was a Jew.

But there is worse to come. Schumann's essay on *Les Huguenots* continues:

> ...It is easy to trace in Meyerbeer Rossini, Mozart, Herold, Weber, Bellini, even Spohr; in short, all there is of music. But one thing belongs to him alone – that famous, unbearably bleating, obscene rhythm, which appears in almost every theme of his opera. I even began to point out the pages where this may be found (pages 6, 17, 59, 68, 77, 100, 117), but finally got enough of it.

Is it not strange that Schumann should have been repulsed by a musical rhythm – to the extent of labeling it "obscene"? Ruth HaCohen has written extensively on what she has termed "the music

---

13. Schumann, *On Music and Musicians*, 126–29.

libel against the Jews."[14] In her book, HaCohen demonstrates how, throughout the ages, anti-Semites have associated certain musical traits (in addition to appearance, gait, odor, speech impediments, etc.) to Jews. Within such a framework, it is tempting to juxtapose the anti-Semitic sentiments expressed in Schumann's marriage diary with this otherwise inexplicable hatred of Meyerbeer (whom he never met), and thus to conclude that Schumann's horrific criticism of *Les Huguenots* was largely dictated by his anti-Semitic sentiments, perhaps exacerbated by his unstable mental condition.[15]

There is another oft-quoted scene in which Schumann overreacted at the mention of Meyerbeer's name. It happened at a dinner party in June 1848, which his wife Clara had organized at the last moment in honor of the pianist Franz Liszt, who had made a surprise visit to Dresden. Referring to Liszt, Alan Walker writes:

> He started to praise Meyerbeer at Mendelssohn's expense. At this, Schumann broke into a violent rage. He sprang up, rushed towards Liszt, seized him by both shoulders, and shouted angrily: "Who are you that you dare to speak in such a way of a musician like Mendelssohn?" He then stalked out of the room, leaving the other dinner-guests staring angrily at Liszt. Liszt rose to the occasion superbly, turned to Clara and said: "Tell your husband that he is the only man in the world from whom I would take so calmly the words just offered to me." Liszt then left the house. Clara declared: "I have done with him forever."[16]

---

14. Ruth HaCohen, *The Music Libel against the Jews* (New Haven: Yale University Press, 2011).
15. Ostwald, *Schumann*, 200–201.
16. Alan Walker, *Franz Liszt*, vol. 2, *The Weimar Years, 1848–1861* (London: Faber and Faber, 1989), 341. Walker details how Liszt tried many times to repair his earlier close friendship with the Schumanns but all to no avail. Even after Robert's death in a mental institution, when Clara fell upon hard times and begrudgingly dared to ask Liszt's help in arranging concerts, Liszt

In public, Meyerbeer generally kept himself aloof from responding to criticism. However, in the case of Schumann's ugly comments about his use of the hymn "Ein Feste Burg," he wrote:

> Actually, this choral serves as a contrast to secular music and is treated in a strict church style, as if it were a voice from a better world, a symbol of hope and faith in the face of threatening danger. It rings out in moments of most glorious inspiration, weaving a thread throughout the entire opera, but only comes from the lips of that individual (the servant Marcel) who, with his simple but unshakable faith, could even be considered a martyr. In view of all this, I would consider its presence in this opera as a glorification rather than a desecration of church music.[17]

Meyerbeer, for his part, in spite of being painfully aware of Schumann's hatred, was still able to appreciate the virtues of the latter's music. For example, in his diary entry for Friday, December 5, 1862, we find:

---

lovingly offered such help. He even arranged other concerts unbidden, but none of this help was ever so much as acknowledged. Clara took her resentment of Liszt with her to the grave. It is also worth pointing out, within the context of this chapter, another fact that Walker emphasizes. Namely, the extremely noble character that Liszt displayed throughout his life even to people who caused him harm. Apparently, at the end of his life, he wrote a very sad letter bemoaning the fact that everyone seemed to have turned against him – "even the Jews, for no reason at all." According to Walker, *Franz Liszt*, 405, a highly anti-Semitic chapter that appeared in a revised version of one of Liszt's books was composed and inserted without the knowledge of the elderly composer by Princess Carolyne Sayn-Wittgenstein, to whom he had entrusted the revision. Liszt was too much of a gentleman to blame her for this scurrilous forgery, preferring to allow his own good name to become besmirched rather than hers.

17. G. Meyerbeer, letter to Gottfried Weber in Darmstadt, October 20, 1837 (English translation by Mark Violette in Becker and Becker, *Giacomo Meyerbeer: A Life in Letters*, 77–79.)

Composer Franz Liszt (1811–1886), who wrote piano compositions based on all of Meyerbeer's grand operas, and who went out of his way to defend the latter's honor in the face of such formidable enemies as Schumann and Wagner; photographed by Franz Hanfstaengl, 1870 (Wikimedia Commons)

...Concert by Robert Radecke: the *Overture, Scherzo and Finale* by Robert Schumann is a very interesting piece of music.[18]

---

18. English translation by Robert Letellier, *The Diaries of Giacomo Meyerbeer*, vol. 4, 279.

Before closing this chapter on the effects of anti-Semitism on Meyerbeer, it is necessary to say a few words about Mendelssohn. Jeffrey Sposato, in a groundbreaking study of that composer's music,[19] has argued that, at least before his father died, Mendelssohn exhibited many examples of anti-Semitism. The phenomenon of former Jews becoming anti-Semites after their conversion to Christianity is of course familiar throughout history and requires no deep psychological explanation. In Mendelssohn's case, such feelings may well have been exacerbated by frustration that he was regarded as a Jew – even by Jews – in spite of the fact that he had not been raised in the religion of his illustrious grandfather, Moses Mendelssohn (1729–1786), and in spite of the fact that after his conversion to Christianity, Felix took his Protestant faith extremely seriously.

However, it is important to realize that his antipathy toward Meyerbeer need not have been a manifestation of anti-Semitism per se. It was probably largely caused by Meyerbeer, the avowed Jew, reminding him of everything he wished to leave behind. It is said that Mendelssohn even cut his hair short when his resemblance to the composer of *Robert le Diable* was pointed out to him by their fellow composer Ferdinand Hiller (1811–1885).[20] It is also not impossible that Mendelssohn felt some pangs of jealousy toward Meyerbeer, brought about by the latter's close working relationship with the Swedish soprano Jenny Lind, of whom the younger composer was apparently extremely fond.[21] Nevertheless, even if Mendelssohn's resentment of Meyerbeer may not have been anti-Semitic in the

---

19. Jeffrey S. Sposato, *The Price of Assimilation: Felix Mendelssohn and the Nineteenth-Century Anti-Semitic Tradition* (Oxford: Oxford University Press, 2006).
20. The circumstances are described by Joseph Bennett in "Giacomo Meyerbeer (1885)," reprinted in Letellier, *Reader*, 200.
21. Clive Brown, *A Portrait of Mendelssohn* (New Haven: Yale University Press, 2003).

conventional sense of Jew hatred, it was certainly an additional reason that Meyerbeer suffered from his own refusal to abandon the religion of his grandfather.[22]

In this chapter, care has been taken to set a background level of racial prejudice, which exists in all societies and at all times, as a bar relative to which statements and actions should be considered in order to decide the extent to which they should or should not be considered anti-Semitic. Against this background that characterized nineteenth-century Europe, it was argued that Beethoven's and Chopin's occasional anti-Semitic remarks were not sufficient for us to regard those composers as anti-Semites. On the other hand, it was demonstrated that Schumann suffered from an inherent anti-Semitism that, coupled with his unfortunate mental instability, was sufficiently strong to totally cloud his judgment of Meyerbeer's opera. Tragically for Meyerbeer, this essay, when first published, evoked vigorous discussion among its many readers and had a widespread influence on public opinion regarding *Les Huguenots* – even though, on musical grounds, it does not fault the opera. One person who was in all probability inspired by Schumann's essay was Richard Wagner, who will now be given a chapter all to himself.

---

22. Robert Letellier points out that because both Mendelssohn and Heine, in spite of being converted Jews, became icons of nineteenth-century culture, their criticisms of Meyerbeer, for whatever reasons each may have had, were as damaging for Meyerbeer's subsequent reputation as were those of the other icons, Schumann and Wagner. Letellier, *The Diaries of Giacomo Meyerbeer*, vol. 1, 50.

Chapter 13

The Case of Richard Wagner

Although it is difficult to give Robert and Clara Schumann the benefit of the doubt and to grant that their antipathy toward Meyerbeer was not racially inspired, no such doubt is possible in the case of Richard Wagner.

A discussion of Wagner is often complicated by the fact that there are really *three* distinct, albeit interrelated, Wagners: there is Wagner the symbol, Wagner the music, and Wagner the man.[1]

Wagner the symbol need not concern us, as it has only an indirect bearing on Meyerbeer. It is discussed in detail in the book *Wagner's Hitler* by Joachim Köhler.[2]

By contrast, Wagner's music has withstood the test of time. Namely, it has outlasted the Wagner "cult" that was created by the composer to promote himself and nurtured by his widow, Cosima, during the many years that she survived him. The music has a powerful effect on most people who hear it. The effect tends to be

---

1. The author wishes to acknowledge Professor Alexander Borg for having helped clarify his perception by pointing out this threefold meaning of the word *Wagner*.
2. Joachim Köhler, *Wagner's Hitler*, ed. and trans. Ronald Taylor (Cambridge, UK: Polity Press, 2000).

one of either adulation or hatred. It is somewhat similar to either liking or not liking Picasso's paintings – but only somewhat. In the case of Wagner's art, it is not usually merely a case of liking it or not liking it. The responses tend to be stronger because his music has the power to excite – positively or negatively – in a manner that is unique among the various art forms. Perhaps it would be more appropriate to liken Wagner's music to a narcotic drug: it either intoxicates people or they refuse to touch the stuff.

The philosopher Friedrich Nietzsche (1844–1900), after many years of idolizing Wagner, ended up by regarding his art as "a disease." Max Nordau (1849–1923), too, who was a pre-Freudian psychoanalyst, regarded Wagner's music as the product of a "degenerate" mind.[3] But nowadays it is pointless to pass judgment on Wagner's music: it is sufficient to observe that within the context of opera, some of his creations are widely held to be among the greatest that have yet been written.

But what about Wagner the man? Clara Schumann, in one of the diary entries to her husband, Robert, observes:

> On the 12th I finally saw 2 acts of the great *Rienzi*, which has driven all of Dresden crazy. I cannot pronounce a judgment about the details after one hearing, but it made an impression on me that I would not seek to have a second time. My entire reaction was displeasure, more I cannot say. The same feeling repeated itself when I got to know Wagner personally; a man who never stops talking about himself, is most arrogant, and constantly laughs in a whining tone.[4]

Note how Clara Schumann took an instinctive dislike to Wagner's music, and then, later, to the man. On the other hand, many other

---

3. Max Nordau, *Degeneration*, translation of the 2nd edition by George L. Mosse (New York: Howard Fertig, 1968), 171–213.
4. Schumann and Schumann, *Marriage Diaries*, 187–88.

people found Wagner's personality absolutely captivating. One such person, who idolized Wagner – at least, to begin with – was Nietzsche. He described his first meeting with Wagner in a manner that in essence is quite similar to Clara's description. However, like the music, Wagner's personality struck a more positive chord with him than with Clara Schumann:

> Wagner conversed wittily in his Saxon dialect, amused the company by parodying characters from his *Meistersinger*, now in his natural pitch, now in falsetto, and recited excerpts from his autobiography.[5]

Readers familiar with the opera *Die Meistersinger von Nürnberg* will have no problem in recognizing the character whom Wagner was said to be parodying in his falsetto voice as Beckmesser. A fact equally well known is that Wagner had originally intended to name this unpleasant character "Hans Lick" because a prominent music critic of the time, Eduard Hanslick (1825–1904), had dared to prefer Brahms's music to Wagner's. However, what is not so well known by modern Wagner lovers is the not-accidental resemblance of Beckmesser to *The Jew among the Thorns* of the Brothers Grimm.[6] But nineteenth-century German audiences would have received the subliminal message from Wagner, associating all that was unpleasant about Beckmesser with the generalized Jewish characteristics that constituted the anti-Semitic stereotype of their time.[7]

Was the use, by Wagner, of this anti-Semitic background merely an indication that Wagner himself was prey to exactly the same prejudices as his peers? That is to say, was Wagner no more of

---

5. Joachim Köhler, *Nietzsche and Wagner: A Lesson in Subjugation*, trans. Ronald Taylor (New Haven: Yale University Press, 1998), 20.
6. The Brothers Grimm, *Complete Fairy Tales*, 528–32.
7. Paul Lawrence Rose, *Wagner: Race and Revolution* (New Haven: Yale University Press, 1992), 112.

an anti-Semite than were Beethoven and Chopin, or even the Schumanns? Here, it will be demonstrated that Wagner's anti-Semitism was of an altogether different rank.

Richard Wagner, composer and anti-Semitic pamphleteer, photographed by Franz Hanfstaengl, 1871 (Wikimedia Commons)

In order to appreciate this strong statement, it is necessary to realize that, in addition to his operas, Wagner wrote an enormous amount of prose, in the form of articles and essays, most of which have been republished in his collected works.[8] In these writings, and to a certain extent, in many of his operas, he espouses a threefold

---

8. Richard Wagner, *Richard Wagner's Prose Works*, trans. William Ashton Ellis, 8 vols. (London: Kegan Paul, 1892–1899).

philosophy: the superiority of the Aryan race, the subservience of the female sex to the needs of the males, and the malignity of the Jewish race.[9] The most notorious among his writings is the essay *Das Judenthum in der Musik* (Jewishness in Music, often translated as "Judaism in Music"), which he first published in 1850 under the pen name "K. Freigedank," and again in 1869 in a slightly expanded form under his own name. The essay caused considerable controversy on both occasions because of its outspoken anti-Semitism. In it Wagner attempts to explain, "scientifically," to his readers, that the repulsion they feel toward Jews is a perfectly natural feeling and, as such, should not be suppressed; that the root cause of this repulsion prevents the Jew from being capable of creating any true art; that Jews, particularly the more cultured among that race, should be pitied for having been born with this eradicable stigma, from which only death can relieve them.

The essay makes extremely difficult reading both because of its odious message and because of Wagner's turgid style of writing. Although it is still a most unpleasant task to go, word by word, through the text, it is important to do so. It should be emphasized that great care has been taken by the present author not to quote Wagner out of context. On the contrary, since *Das Judenthum* is structured toward discrediting the music of Mendelssohn and Meyerbeer, all quotations are given, in the order in which Wagner enunciates them: first those passages in which Wagner expounds his racial argument, followed by his use of this argument to dismiss

---

9. The threefold philosophy that underlies most of Wagner's oeuvre has been emphasized by the composer's great-grandson, Gottfried Wagner, in, for example, "On the Need to Debate Richard Wagner in an Open Society: How to Confront Wagner Today beyond Glorification and Condemnation," in *Richard Wagner for the New Millenium*, eds. Matthew Bribitzer-Stull, Alex Lubet, and Gottfried Wagner (New York: Palgrave Macmillan, 2007), 3–24.

any mistaken notions his readers may have as to the artistic worth of these two eminent Jewish composers – particularly Meyerbeer.

Das Judenthum is not the only essay in which Wagner attacks Jews for having corrupted true art by their, according to him, racially embedded avariciousness. He does so in his 1878 *Was ist Deutsch* (What is German) and in other writings. However, *Das Judenthum* has a specific aim: namely, to discredit the music of the two composers whom Wagner regarded as his most serious rivals, and this he does by a malicious manipulation of the anti-Semitic sentiments of his readers against these particular composers because of their Jewishness. Wagner's argument begins thus:

> The Jew – who, as everyone knows, has a God all to himself – in ordinary life strikes us primarily by his outward appearance, which, no matter to what European nationality we belong, has something disagreeably foreign to that nationality: instinctively we wish to have nothing in common with a man who looks like that.... Passing over the moral side, in the effect of this in itself unpleasant freak of Nature, and coming to its bearings upon Art, we here will merely observe that to us this exterior can never be thinkable as a subject for the art of re-presentment: ... But the Jew never wanders on to the theatric boards: ... We can conceive no representation of an antique or modern stage-character by a Jew, be it as hero or lover, without feeling instinctively the incongruity of such a notion.

Notice how Wagner verbalizes feelings which he is suggesting the reader shares with him – by use of the first person plural form – about what he describes as an "unpleasant freak of nature," deducing that such a visually ugly character could never be the subject of any visual artistic creation. (Amusingly, Wagner was later to lean on this argument to try to attribute Aryan ancestry to the biblical Jesus!)

Having dispensed with looks, he then goes on to sounds:

> By far more weighty, nay, of quite decisive weight for our inquiry, is the effect the Jew produces on us through his speech....
>
> In particular does the purely physical aspect of the Jewish mode of speech repel us.... The first thing that strikes our ear as quite outlandish and unpleasant, in the Jew's production of the voice-sounds, is a creaking, squeaking, buzzing snuffle:... the cold indifference of its peculiar "blubber" ["Gelabber"] never by any chance rises to the ardour of a higher, heartfelt passion.

If this is reminiscent of Nietzsche's description of Wagner employing a falsetto voice to parody a character in *Meistersinger*, it is not coincidental. This is the kind of voice that Wagner's stage instructions provide for the characters Alberich and Mime in his opera tetralogy, *Der Ring des Nibelungen*.[10] Like Beckmesser in *Meistersinger*, they are not Jews, but these sound effects would, with Wagner's help, reach into the subconscious of his nineteenth-century audiences, evoking feelings of appropriate revulsion.

From speech, Wagner moves on to song and music, and, as if all of his readers are familiar with a synagogue service, he rants:

> ...Who has not had occasion to convince himself of the travesty of a divine service of song, presented in a real Folk-synagogue? Who has not been seized with a feeling of the greatest revulsion, of horror mingled with the absurd, at hearing that sense-and-sound-confounding gurgle, yodel and cackle, which no intentional caricature can make more repugnant than as offered here in full, in naive seriousness?

Having thus employed, like Schumann, the music libel[11] to round off the setting he has created, Wagner then poses the question:

---

10. Marc A. Weiner, *Richard Wagner and the Anti-Semitic Imagination* (Lincoln: University of Nebraska Press, 1997), 143–46.
11. HaCohen, *The Music Libel against the Jews*.

If the Jew is so incapable of creating any kind of art, how does it happen that he is so involved in it? Naturally, Wagner has the answer ready:

> ...To explain to ourselves this phenomenon...the Jews not merely could no longer be denied the diploma of a new society that needed naught but gold, but they brought it with them in their pockets. Wherefore our modern Culture, accessible to no one but the well-to-do, remained the less a closed book to them, as it had sunk into a venal article of Luxury.
>
> ...The cultured Jew has taken the most indicible pains to strip off all the obvious tokens of his lower co-religionists: in many a case he has even held it wise to make a Christian baptism wash away the traces of his origin.... Now, our modern arts had likewise become a portion of this culture, and among them more particularly that art which is just the very easiest to learn – the art of music...

A Christian baptism is his first allusion to Mendelssohn, but worse is to come. However, before analyzing Wagner's dismissal of Mendelssohn's art, the sentences that follow immediately after the previous quotation are particularly revealing:

> and indeed that Music which, severed from her sister arts, had been lifted by the force and stress of grandest geniuses to a stage in her universal faculty of Expression where either, in new conjunction with the other arts, she might speak aloud the most sublime, or, in persistent separation from them, she could also speak at will the deepest bathos of the trivial. Naturally, what the cultured Jew had to speak, in his aforesaid situation, could be nothing but the trivial and indifferent.... At present no art affords such plenteous possibility of talking in it without saying any real thing, as that of Music, since the greatest geniuses have already said whatever there was to say in it as an absolute separate-art.

What Wagner is saying is that the greatest geniuses of the past, specifically Bach, Mozart, and Beethoven, have written everything that music is capable of expressing on its own. Any further attempts to compose music for its own sake – as opposed to music in combination with the other arts (of which Wagner was claiming to be the supreme exponent) – could only lead to artistic trivialities. Here, he was taking his first swipe at Mendelssohn (and on the side, also at Brahms and Schumann, who, albeit not Jews, were equal causes of jealousy for him). However, now comes his direct attack on Mendelssohn:

> By what example will this all grow clearer to us – ay, well nigh what other single case could make us so alive to it, as the works of a musician of Jewish birth whom Nature had endowed with specific musical gifts as very few before him? All that offered itself to our gaze, in the inquiry into our antipathy against the Jewish nature; all the contradictoriness of this nature, both in itself and as touching us; all its inability, while outside our footing, to have intercourse with us upon that footing, nay, even to form a wish to further develop the things which had sprung from out our soil: all these are intensified to a positively tragic conflict in the nature, life, and art-career of the early-taken FELIX MENDELSSOHN BARTHOLDY. He has shewn us that a Jew may have the amplest store of specific talents, may own the finest and most varied culture, the highest and the tenderest sense of honour – yet without all these pre-eminences helping him, were it but one single time, to call forth in us that deep, that heart-searching effect which we await from Art [24] because we know her capable thereof, because we have felt it many a time and oft, so soon as once a hero of our art has, so to say, but opened his mouth to speak to us. To professional critics, who haply have reached a like consciousness with ourselves hereon, it may be left to prove by specimens of Mendelssohn's art-products our statement of this indubitably certain thing...

Although this quotation speaks for itself, three comments are in order. The first is Wagner's emphasis that Mendelssohn's Jewish birth, not his conversion to and practice of Christianity, prevents him from ever being a true artist. Second is Wagner's oratorial trick of not making a frontal attack on what his readers had no doubt previously believed. After all, Mendelssohn was widely held, all over Germany and in much of the rest of the musical world, to have inherited the mantle of Beethoven. The remarks of Robert and Clara Schumann, illustrated in the previous chapter, in another context, are but two examples of deep respect for Mendelssohn's music. Instead, Wagner goes along with his readers' presumed admiration of Mendelssohn, skillfully steering it so as to convince them that it is simply Mendelssohn's technical skill, and not his nonexistent art, that so charms everyone, *including himself*. The third comment to note is that Wagner does not try to explain what is false about Mendelssohn's art. Instead he states it as an obvious fact that all technical experts would have reached the same conclusion. In hindsight, we may well ask: But how did those technical experts react to having this assertion placed on their lips? This question will be returned to later, when it will be shown how at least one prominent early twentieth-century music critic and lover of Meyerbeer's operas was simply too scared to swim against the stream.

But now it is Meyerbeer's turn to suffer Wagner's wrath. Wagner's attack on Meyerbeer needed heavier artillery than that on Mendelssohn, because the latter was not revered as a composer of operas. It was only his phenomenal musical abilities that made Wagner jealous. In fact, in one of his dreams, related by his widow, Cosima, Wagner saw Mendelssohn standing next to him at the piano and laughing at his attempt to orchestrate one of his operas. Equally frustrating was the fact that, unlike Wagner's, Meyerbeer's operas were big-time box-office the world over. It has been estimated that the royalties from his operas were enough to make him a multimillionaire in modern terms. So, how does Wagner criticize Meyerbeer? Thusly:

> A like sympathy, however, can no other Jew composer rouse in us. A far-famed Jewish tone-setter of our day has addressed himself and products to a section of our public whose total confusion of musical taste was less to be first caused by him, than worked out to his profit. The public of our Opera-theatre of nowadays has for long been gradually led aside from those claims which rightly should be addressed, not only to the Dramatic Artwork, but in general to every work of healthy taste. The places in our halls of entertainment are mostly filled by nothing but that section of our citizen society whose only ground for change of occupation is utter 'boredom' (Langeweile): the disease of boredom, however, is not remediable by sips of Art; for it can never be distracted of set purpose, but merely duped into another form of boredom. Now, the catering for this deception that famous opera-composer has made the task of his artistic life.

At this point, Wagner introduces the following footnote: "Whoever has observed the shameful indifference and absent-mindedness of a Jewish congregation, throughout the musical performance of Divine Service in the Synagogue, may understand why a Jewish opera-composer feels not at all offended by encountering the same thing in a theatre-audience, and how he cheerfully can go on labouring for it; for this behaviour, here, must really seem to him less unbecoming than in the house of God."

> There is no object in more closely designating the artistic means he has expended on the reaching of this life's-aim: enough that, as we may see by the result, he knew completely how to dupe; and more particularly by taking that jargon which we have already characterised, and palming it upon his ennuyed audience as the modern-piquant utterance of all the trivialities which so often had been set before them in all their natural foolishness. That this composer took also thought for thrilling situations (Erschütterungen) and the effective weaving of emotional catastrophes

(Gefühlskatastrophen), need astonish none who know how necessarily this sort of thing is wished by those whose time hangs heavily upon their hands; nor need any wonder that in this his aim succeeded too, if they but will ponder well the reasons why, in such conditions, the whole was bound to prosper with him. In fact, this composer pushes his deception so far, that he ends by deceiving himself, and perchance as purposely as he deceives his bored admirers. We believe, indeed, that he honestly would like to turn out artworks, and yet is well aware he cannot: to extricate himself from this painful conflict between Will and Can, he writes operas for Paris, and sends them touring round the world – the surest means, to-day, of earning oneself an art renown albeit not an artist. Under the burden of this self-deception, which may not be so toilless as one might think, he, too, appears to us wellnigh in a tragic light: yet the purely personal element of wounded vanity turns the thing into a tragi-comedy, just as in general the un-inspiring, the truly laughable, is the characteristic mark whereby this famed composer shews his Jewhood in his music.

From a closer survey of the instances adduced above – which we have learnt to grasp by getting to the bottom of our indomitable objection to the Jewish nature – there more especially results for us a proof of the ineptitude of the present musical epoch. Had the two aforesaid Jew composers [see Wagner's footnote below] in truth helped Music into riper bloom, then we should merely have had to admit that our tarrying behind them rested on some organic debility that had taken sudden hold of us: but not so is the case; on the contrary, as compared with bygone epochs, the specific musical powers of nowadays have rather increased than diminished. The incapacity lies in the spirit of our Art itself, which is longing for another life than the artificial one now toilsomely upheld for it. The incapacity of the musical art variety, itself, is exposed for us in the art-doings of Mendelssohn, the uncommonly-gifted specific musician; but the nullity of our whole public system, its utterly un-artistic claims and nature, in the successes of that famous Jewish opera-composer grow clear for anyone to see. These are the weighty points that have now to draw towards themselves the whole attention of everyone who means honestly by Art...

As with Wagner's tirade against Mendelssohn, no criticism of Meyerbeer's operas is made on musical grounds. It is all on racial grounds ("which we have learnt to grasp by getting to the bottom of our indomitable objection to the Jewish nature") within the context that he has carefully set up in the foregoing. Notice that Wagner is so disgusted with "that famous Jewish opera-composer" that he never even deigns to mention him by name. In the last of this set of paragraphs Wagner inserts a second footnote, cunningly aimed at his Jewish readers, most of whom would not be inclined to accept his racial slurs. It reads:

> Characteristic enough is the attitude adopted by the remaining Jew musicians, nay, by the whole of cultured Jewry, toward their two most renowned composers. To the adherents of Mendelssohn, that famous opera-composer is an atrocity: with a keen sense of honour, they feel how much he compromises Jewdom in the eyes of better trained musicians, and therefore shew no mercy in their judgment. By far more cautiously do that composer's retainers express themselves concerning Mendelssohn, regarding more with envy, than with manifest ill-will, the success he has made in the "more solid" music-world. To a third faction, that of the composition-at-any-price Jews, it is their visible object to avoid all internecine scandal, all self-exposure in general, so that their music-producing may take its even course without occasioning any painful fuss: the by all means undeniable successes of the great opera-composer they let pass as worth some slight attention, allowing there is something in them albeit one

can't approve of much or dub it "solid." In sooth, the Jews are far too clever, not to know how their own goods are lined!

This footnote arguably did more lasting damage to Meyerbeer's reputation than everything else that was written about him. After all, the Jews were among Wagner's most ardent supporters, and it was of the utmost importance to him that they should remain that way and not revert to any former esteem they would doubtlessly have held for Meyerbeer's operas. What he was telling them was: *I can well understand your misguided love of Mendelssohn's music, on account of the racial impediment with which you were all born. However, even you people have enough sensitivity to realize what utter trash that famous composer of operas wrote.*

Why more damage than anything else? First, by the time *Das Judenthum* received its second publication, Wagner's musical reputation was so high that he was well on the way to becoming the center of a "cult." Furthermore, it was a cult to which Jews, particularly German Jews, clamored for entry. So, if denigrating Meyerbeer was part of the entrance fee, then it was an acceptable price. In any case, the operatic style of *Robert le Diable* was rather old-fashioned compared to their great master's "music of the future."

But for Jews, as many were tragically to demonstrate in the suicide notes they left behind, entry into the cult of Wagnerism was a perilous journey. The closing sentence of *Das Judenthum* explains why:

> To become Man at once with us, however, means firstly for the Jew as much as ceasing to be Jew.... But bethink ye, that one only thing can redeem you from the burden of your curse: the redemption of Ahasuerus – Going under!

Ahasuerus here is not the Persian king in the biblical Book of Esther, who ultimately modified his original deadly decree by permitting the Jews to defend themselves. Instead, Wagner is here alluding to the

Wandering Jew, as depicted in ancient German legend, whose curse – to wander the Earth until the end of time – can only be redeemed by death. He appears as the mysterious Dutchman in Wagner's early opera *Der fliegende Holländer* and as Kundry in *Parsifal*, his last opera. The philosopher Otto Weininger (1880–1903) was only one of many Jewish unfortunates who became so besotted with the Wagner cult as to take his own life.[12]

Attempts are often made by Wagner lovers – who have doubtless not studied *Das Judenthum in der Musik* – to downgrade the composer's outspoken anti-Semitism by claiming that it pales into insignificance compared to the overall behavior of this thoroughly amoral person. He lived a life of luxury at other people's expense, borrowing and spending their money lavishly and skipping town when necessary in order to escape the debt collectors. Nietzsche describes having been sent on errands by "the master" to purchase everything from expensive silk underwear to a chandelier that the architect Gottfried Semper had promised the Jewish community of Dresden for the magnificent new synagogue he had designed for them.[13]

Wagner was also an unashamed hypocrite. At the time of the 1848 revolution that swept Europe, he urged personal friends to man the street barricades against charging royal soldiers, while he kept himself safely out of harm's way. On the other hand, he happily accepted royal patronage from Ludwig, king of Bavaria, ostensibly to enable him to build a unique opera house at Bayreuth. But this same source of money also funded the lavish villa, "Wahnfried," that Wagner built for himself, together with all the luxury goods he required Nietzsche and other acolytes to purchase for him. And

---

12. Otto Weininger, *Sex and Character: An Investigation of Fundamental Principles*, trans. Ladislaus Loeb (Bloomington: Indiana University Press, 2005). See particularly chapter 13, "Judaism," 272ff.
13. Köhler, *Nietzsche and Wagner*, 61–62.

if he availed himself of his friends' money, he was equally free with their wives. He had many trysts while married to his first wife Minna, and Cosima von Bülow, who became his second wife, actually bore him three children before her first husband realized what was going on. How could such a thing happen? Simply because the famous conductor Hans von Bülow so idolized Wagner and his music that he went around the world spreading the master's gospel while the master stayed home looking after the conductor's neglected wife!

With such an attitude to right and wrong, one should not be surprised that Wagner adopted as his own many musical devices of others. Perhaps the two most notorious examples are the piece of Mendelssohn's *Reformation Symphony* that appears in *Parsifal*, and his stealing from Meyerbeer the credit for having created what Wagner referred to as the *Gesamptkunstwerk* (total artwork). Of course, it was not in Meyerbeer's nature to proclaim any such lofty principle about his own grand operas. However, a leading philosopher-critic of his day, Joseph d'Ortigue (1802–1866),[14] pointed out that Meyerbeer's successful combination of all the arts in *Robert le Diable* had finally brought about his (d'Ortigue's) long wished-for "total work of art" – a full generation before Wagner claimed to have invented the concept.

No wonder then that Wagner felt the need to remove these two Jews from their rightful place in the history of music, by trashing their reputations. And for this purpose, even if one wishes to believe the myth that Wagner was not himself an anti-Semite (and myth it is),[15] he certainly knew how to use the anti-Semitism of others to

---

14. Joseph d'Ortigue in *Le Balcon de l'opéra*, quoted by Matthias Brzoska in his 2004 lecture "The Central Philosophical Ideas of Meyerbeer's Conception of Historical Grand Opera, and Especially *Le Prophète* – The Genesis of the Work and the Principles of the New Edition," reprinted in Letellier, *Reader*, 603–4.

15. Joachim Köhler, in his book *Wagner's Hitler*, provides copious quotations

promote his aims. In so doing he was enormously successful. For at least half a century following Wagner's death, Mendelssohn's music came to be regarded as a shallow imitation of that of the great masters who had preceded him, and Meyerbeer's reputation as a composer of operas was totally destroyed. Do such actions really pale into insignificance compared to Wagner's other manifestations of amoral behavior? After all, if we are to enjoy Wagner's music, should we not be allowed to enjoy all the sources from which it came, both "Aryan" and others?

---

from Wagner's private correspondence with his patron, King Ludwig of Bavaria. There one finds blatantly anti-Semitic statements such as (p. 317): "Nature is created in such a way that wherever a parasite sees its advantage, there it will settle. A dying body will attract these maggots, which will ultimately destroy the host and assimilate with it. This is precisely the role of the Jews in modern European culture." This is not Wagner trying to destroy the reputation of two rival musicians: it is Wagner attempting to coax a king into outlawing an entire nation. These letters demonstrate that there is no way of absolving Wagner from the charge of being an active and dangerous anti-Semite.

Chapter 14
Meyerbeer in Israel

Meyerbeer, as we have seen, was an avowed Jew who suffered from anti-Semitism all his life. It would accordingly seem perfectly understandable if his compositions had remained a staple part of the repertoire, at least in the country that has long been designated as a homeland for the Jewish people. After all, the music of Mendelssohn, who did not remain a Jew after his formal conversion to Christianity at the age of sixteen, is widely performed in Israel, and also by Israeli musicians in their overseas concerts. Remarkably, this is not the case with Meyerbeer, the Jew who did not convert out – a mystery that can only be understood as the lingering effect on music lovers to this day of Wagner's malignant philosophy.

This chapter outlines the development of so-called "classical" music in Israel, and the honorable place that some of the founding fathers gave Meyerbeer. Before doing so, however, there is a small geo-historical obstacle that must be cleared up, because, although the modern State of Israel only came into being in 1948, the preparations for a state, including its musical institutions, had actually begun a half century or so earlier.

Before the First World War (1914–1918), the modern countries of Israel, Jordan, Lebanon, Syria, and Iraq were all part of the former Ottoman Empire, with no clearly defined borders to distinguish

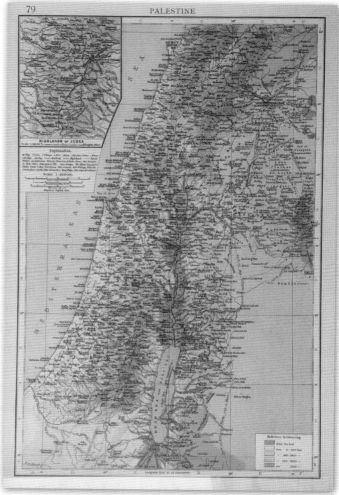

A map of Palestine from the year 1900, typical of the pre-WWI era, showing the River Jordan in the center, and including parts of modern Israel, Jordan, Lebanon, and Syria (David Faiman collection)

among them. Nevertheless, European atlases usually contained a map of "Palestine," the sites with biblical associations being marked for the assistance of Bible readers, pilgrims, and other interested travelers. These maps, as typified by an example from the 1900 edition of the *Times Atlas*, place the River Jordan at the center of the country and include modern Israel and Jordan, together with the cities Beirut (in modern Lebanon) and Damascus (in modern Syria).

Constantinople was the capital of the Ottoman Empire, and its opera house performed all four of Meyerbeer's grand operas as well as *Dinorah*.[1] There is no indication that the further reaches of the empire enjoyed the luxury of an opera house: certainly not its eastern edge, where Palestine was to be found. Constantinople had a sizeable Jewish population: some 65,000 according to one pre-WWI source, but the empire's next largest concentration of Jews, 48,400, was in Jerusalem.[2]

Apart from the relatively small number of Jews who had remained in the Holy Land since Roman times, principally in Jerusalem, Safed, Tiberias, and Hebron, Jerusalem had become the final resting place to which many elderly non-Palestinian Jews would retire to live out their final days. However, Jewish immigration from Europe received a new boost with the publication of Theodor Herzl's *The Jewish State* in 1896, and the sequence of annual Zionist Congresses that commenced a year later starting in Basel, Switzerland, and continuing in various other European cities.

Western classical music naturally played an important role in the Zionist culture because most of the newcomers had benefited from a European or Russian education. For example, as early as 1895, a small symphony orchestra was founded in the agricultural settlement of Rishon leZion.[3] The orchestra soon invoked the ire of Moshe Lilienblum, a political leader who objected to pioneers

---

1. Alfred Loewenberg, *Annals of Opera, 1597–1940* (Cambridge, UK: W. Heffer and Sons, 1943), 371, 394, 445, 482, 498.
2. "Jewish Chronicle" Year Book: *An Annual Record of Matters Jewish, 5671–72* (London, 1911), 270–72.
3. Jehoash Hirshberg, *Music in the Jewish Community of Palestine, 1880–1948* (Oxford: Oxford University Press, 2002), 25–28.

wasting their time on such an idle pursuit as music when there were fields to be cleared of stones and crops to be planted. Jehoash Hirshberg, in his book *Music in the Jewish Community of Palestine, 1880–1948*, quotes a sarcastic response to Lilienblum published by one of the orchestra's members:

> There are 168 hours per week, of which we waste – that is, a few of us, who have the talent – six hours in refreshing our souls with the sweetness of the great spirits, of the giant spirits: Halévy, Meyerbeer, Mendelssohn, Beethoven, Mozart, Wagner, and so on....[4]

This extract indicates that even in this far-flung part of the nineteenth-century Ottoman Empire, Meyerbeer's name was still mentioned in the same sentence as those composers whose reputations were not to undergo the decline that did his. However, there are three telling observations regarding this quotation that we can make with the benefit of hindsight: first, that the anonymous writer grouped the three "Jewish" composers at the beginning, no doubt to impress Lilienblum, whom he clearly regarded as a cultural philistine; second, that Wagner is included as one of the three non-Jewish "giant spirits"; third, that even Lilienblum (whatever his cultural inclinations) would have been expected by the writer to recognize the name Meyerbeer.

According to Hirshberg, even the fiftieth anniversary of Meyerbeer's death was commemorated by a special concert on May 13, 1914. However, it was not the farmers' orchestra from Rishon leZion who organized that concert but, rather, the faculty and pupils of Palestine's first music conservatory, which had been founded in 1910 in Jaffa by Shulamith Ruppin.

So, up until the year 1914, there was still apparently no indication of any decline in the popularity of Meyerbeer among music lovers

---

4. Hirshberg, *Music in the Jewish Community of Palestine*, 25–28.

in Palestine. But in 1914, WWI broke out, and Jewish life in the country was severely disrupted. Jews who were unwilling to take up Ottoman citizenship were deported, mostly to Egypt, and those who remained were given more pressing duties than playing music.

With the defeat of Turkey and its allies in 1918 came the start of a thirty-year British occupation of Palestine. All kinds of matters that had previously been rather ill-defined under Ottoman rule were put in order. For example, the map of Palestine was now given new and well-defined boundaries: The country was henceforth to extend only from the Mediterranean Sea to the River Jordan. All the rest of the territory that was mandated to Britain by the League of Nations was defined as "Transjordan." (Beirut in Lebanon and Damascus in Syria lay outside of Britain's mandate.)

It may be recalled that the so-called "Balfour Declaration," which had been issued by Britain in 1917, designated the establishment of a home for the Jewish people in *Palestine*. So, under British administration, just to make matters clear, Jewish settlement was permitted only within the newly defined boundaries of the country.[5] Moreover, even the postage stamps, issued by His Majesty's Government for use in the reduced Palestine, named the county in English, Hebrew, and Arabic, whereas those issued for the newly created Transjordan excluded any Hebrew inscription.[6]

Naturally, with the termination of WWI, cultural life resumed in Palestine, and considerable numbers of Jews who had been exiled by the Ottoman authorities returned to their homes in various parts of

---

5. Michael J. Cohen, *Britain's Moment in Palestine: Retrospect and Perspectives, 1917–48* (Abingdon, UK: Routledge, 2014), 130.
6. Donald M. Reid, "The Symbolism of Postage Stamps: A Source for the Historian," in *Journal of Contemporary History* 19, no. 2 (1984): 223–49. In this widely cited paper, Reid argues that postage stamps represent the government's official stand on what they depict.

Official postage stamps issued by Great Britain in 1927 for use in Palestine. They depict various sites in the country and bear inscriptions in English, Hebrew, and Arabic. The three examples shown here were franked at post offices in Gaza, Hebron, and Jericho, respectively. (David Faiman collection)

the country, including Tel Aviv, which had been founded only five years before the outbreak of war.

In 1922, the British authorities conducted their first official census of the population.[7] By that time, the Jewish population was found to comprise some 84,000. The largest communities, in descending order of size, were in Jerusalem, Tel Aviv, Haifa, Jaffa, Tiberias, Petah Tikva, Safed, Rishon leZion, Rehovot, and Zichron Yaakov. Smaller communities (i.e., fewer than a thousand residents) were scattered among other towns, including Hebron (430), Beersheba (98), and Gaza (54), with a few Jews living as far from the Mediterranean coast as Jericho. At that time the kibbutz movement, which had started with the founding of Degania as recently as 1909, totaled only seven hundred souls.[8]

---

7. J.B. Barron, *Palestine: Report and General Abstracts of the Census of 1922* (Jerusalem: Greek Convent Press, 1922).
8. Nahum Sokolow, *History of Zionism, 1600–1918*, vol. 2 (London: Longmans, Green, 1919), 326–27.

Having reviewed this brief overview of the geography and musical history of Palestine,[9] let us now return to opera and Meyerbeer.

In 1923 a most remarkable man arrived in Palestine. His name was Mordechai Golinkin, an opera conductor from St. Petersburg. While still in Russia, Golinkin had published a manifesto in which he had called for the founding, in Jerusalem, of a Hebrew "Temple of Art."[10] He argued that the Italians had their La Scala, and the Germans their Bayreuth. So it was only natural, if Jews were truly to renew their ancient musical heritage, for them to establish such a temple in Jerusalem. Golinkin, having arrived from post-revolution Russia, outlined a kibbutz-like community, in which children would be educated in all of the arts from a young age, and where those with outstanding talent would have their specific gifts nurtured. The temple would have a touring orchestra that would play free concerts around the country for the workers. In such an atmosphere, he believed, native Hebrew culture would revive, reaching a par with that of the other nations, and indigenous Hebrew opera would emerge.

Golinkin's manifesto was widely hailed by the Zionist intellectuals of Palestine, a delegation of whom turned out to greet this visionary upon his arrival at the port of Jaffa. When asked to be taken to their opera house, Golinkin received his first sad shock. For, at that time, postwar Palestine was riven with poverty and disease: an opera house was the last kind of institution that anyone had ever thought

---

9. This musical review is far from complete in that it aims to serve as an introduction to Meyerbeer's music in the country. To this end it has emphasized to the exclusion of all else the introduction of Western classical music. It has ignored the riches of local Arabic music and the musical traditions of the many oriental Jewish communities who had settled in pre-WWI Palestine.
10. Mordechai Golinkin, *Mi-Heichalei Yefet l'Ohalei Shem* (From the Temples of Japheth to the Tents of Shem) [In Hebrew] (Tel Aviv: privately published, 1957).

Conductor Mordechai Golinkin (1875–1963), who established the Palestine Opera in 1923 (Mordechai Golinkin, Mi-Heichalei Yefet l'Ohalei Shem, *1957)*

about![11] But Golinkin, before leaving Russia, had, together with his friend the famous singer Feodor Chaliapin, given a benefit concert to help him get an opera company started in Jerusalem. So, to that city, he set out. There, he encountered a childhood friend, who was eking out a living by giving music lessons and repairing instruments. He advised the famous conductor to return to Jaffa, rather than

---

11. Peter Gradenwitz, in *The Music of Israel from the Biblical Era to Modern Times*, 2nd ed. (Portland, OR: Amadeus Press, 1996), 324, claims that an abortive attempt to found an opera company had been made a year before by Sir Ronald Storrs, the military governor of Jerusalem.

Operatic bass Feodor Chaliapin (1873–1938), who concertized in Russia to help Mordechai Golinkin raise money to start an opera in Palestine; photographed before 1930 (Wikimedia Commons)

Jerusalem, because there Shulamith Ruppin's conservatory might be able to provide him with instrumentalists and singers.

Incredibly, against all odds, Mordechai Golinkin was able to found the Palestine Opera the very same year of his arrival in the country. For an opera house he was allowed to use Jaffa's Eden cinema – but with a severe restriction. Apparently, there was one evening a week in which no films were screened, and that was the only evening in which Golinkin could use the building. To do so, he and his troupe had to remove most of the seats, perform their rehearsal, and then restore the cinema to a state that would be ready for the next night's screening.

The Eden Cinema in Jaffa, where the Palestine Opera rehearsed its productions (photo courtesy of Leah Etzion)

But that was the least of Golinkin's problems. His orchestra and chorus comprised students from the conservatory, all of whom had various jobs during the day in order to support themselves. He had, accordingly, to seek them out during their respective spare hours and perform partial rehearsals with as many as he could assemble at any given time. Only once a week could they all come together for a joint rehearsal.

His soloists comprised various adults who had received some musical training before coming to Palestine, and a number of visiting artists. The final complication was that Golinkin insisted that all operas must be performed in Hebrew – a language that neither he nor most of the visiting artists could understand!

And the result? Believe it or not, the 1923 "season" – i.e., the very year in which Golinkin arrived – staged no fewer than six different operas: Verdi's *La Traviata* and *Rigoletto*, Leoncavallo's *I Pagliacci*; Gounod's *Faust* and *Romeo et Juliette*; and Halévy's *La Juive*!

In addition to insisting that all performances be in the Hebrew language, Golinkin also inserted into each year's program one opera with an explicitly Hebrew motive: thus, Halévy's *La Juive* that first year – a work that got him into trouble with the local ecclesiastical authorities. During the 1924 season, the Palestine opera staged six more operas, which included *Samson et Dalila* of Saint-Saëns as that year's "Jewish" feature. The 1925 season witnessed three new operas, which included *Die Maccabäer* of Anton Rubinstein. Finally, being by that time in dire financial straits, the Palestine Opera's 1926 season consisted of only two works: Meyerbeer's *Les Huguenots* (Hebrew translation by Aharon Ashman) and Rossini's *Il barbiere di Siviglia*.

With that, the company declared bankruptcy. They had staged seventeen different operas around the country, playing everywhere to packed houses – large parts of the audiences, according to newspaper reports, standing outside to at least hear the music. But, as is well known the world over, opera then as now cannot survive without heavy government subsidy, and British Palestine of the 1920s could not provide such a luxury. On the contrary, the authorities even exacted an "entertainments tax" on the tickets! Some further details of Golinkin's seventeen Hebrew-language operatic productions are given in appendix 4.

Regarding *Les Huguenots*, as indicated by contemporary newspaper advertisements, the opera was terminated at the end of act 4 – but well after midnight, according to the reviews. Eleven performances were given on the dates and venues listed in table 1.

The cast for *Les Huguenots* is given in table 2. Unfortunately, neither first names nor initials were given in the newspaper advertisements or program notes. Those few that are included in the table have been gleaned from various other sources, mostly from Golinkin's two books.[12]

---

12. Golinkin, *Mi-Heichalei Yefet l'Ohalei Shem*; Mordechai Golinkin, *The Temple of Art* [in English] (Tel Aviv, 1957).

Table 1: Dates and venues of *Les Huguenots* performances by the Palestine Opera (from newspaper advertisements)

Date	Theater	Town
Thursday, December 9, 1926	Eden	Tel Aviv*
Monday, December 13, 1926	Zion	Jerusalem
Tuesday, December 14, 1926	Zion	Jerusalem
Thursday, December 16, 1926	Eden	Tel Aviv
Thursday, December 30, 1926	Eden	Tel Aviv
Tuesday, January 4, 1927	Zion	Jerusalem
Thursday, January 6, 1927	Eden	Tel Aviv
Thursday, January 13, 1927	Herzlia	Petah Tikva
Saturday, January 15, 1927	Herzlia	Petah Tikva
Tuesday, January 8, 1927	Eden	Haifa
Thursday, January 17, 1927	Eden	Tel Aviv

* The December 9, 1926, performance in Tel Aviv was presumably a public dress rehearsal.

Very little is known about most of these singers. However, bass Matvey Goryainov had previously recorded Marcel's "Piff, paff, piff, paff!" aria. Moreover, tenor Arnon Rojansky, one of Golinkin's troup who did not take part in *Les Huguenots*, also left a professional recording – of "Land, so wunderbar" from *L'Africaine*.[13]

Of the Jerusalem opening, the English-language *Palestine Bulletin* included the following review:

---

13. Arsenty and Letellier, *Giacomo Meyerbeer: A Discography*, 136, states that a ten-inch record of Goryainov was issued around 1902 on the Zonofon label, with matrix no. X-62522; p. 211 states that a ten-inch record of Rojansky was issued on the Artiphon label, with record no. 11562. The latter, with Rojansky singing in Hebrew, may be heard at https://www.youtube.com/watch?v=IUi6oMenahc.

Table 2: Cast list of *Les Huguenots*, as performed by the Palestine Opera, 1926–27

Character	Singer
Marguerite de Valois, queen of Navarre	Mrs. Ruth Leviash (soprano)
Valentine, daughter of the comte de Saint-Bris	Mrs. L. Golinkin[14] (soprano)
Urbain, the queen's page	Mrs. S. Krieger (mezzo-soprano)
Two ladies in waiting to the queen	Mrs. Wasserman (soprano) Mrs. Bahrav (soprano)
Raoul de Nangis, a Protestant gentleman	Mr. G. Giorini (tenor)
De Tavannes, a Catholic gentleman	Mr. Lilienblum (tenor)
De Cossé, ditto	Mr. Mindlin (tenor)
De Thoré, ditto	Mr. Milstein (bass)
Le comte de Nevers, ditto	Mr. M. Konstantinovsky (baritone)
Le comte de Saint-Bris, ditto	Mr. Moshe Rudinow (bass)
De Retz, ditto	Mr. Gindin (bass)
Maurevert, ditto	Mr. Savransky (baritone)
Marcel, a Huguenot soldier, Raoul's servant	Mr. M. Goryainov (bass)

A representative audience assembled last night for the opening of the Jerusalem Opera season in Zion Hall, when the "Huguenots" by Meyerbeer was performed. Practically all the members of the company appeared in the opera. The main solo as well as the ensemble parts were sung excellently. The enlarged chorus, the orchestra and the ballet showed great progress. The audience was charmed. There was an ovation for Mr. Golinkin, the Director, and the whole company.[15]

---

14. The conductor's second wife, L. Golinkin (photo in his 1957 book *The Temple of Art*); his first wife, Miriam (photos in his 1931 book *Mi-Heichalei Yefet l'Ohalei Shem*).

15. *The Palestine Bulletin*, December 14, 1926, 3.

By contrast, letters to the editor in the Hebrew-language press were less complimentary. They made little reference, if at all, to either music or staging. What drew their ire was what they described as "terrible Hebrew"! It must be recalled that in those days, revival of the ancient Hebrew language was the uppermost cultural task in the minds of the Jewish community of Palestine.

A more positive assessment of the Palestine Opera came from no less a dignitary than Sir Herbert Samuel, the first High Commissioner of Palestine. In a report on the administration of the country from 1920 to 1925 to the Permanent Mandates Commission of the League of Nations, he wrote:

> Not least interesting among these developments is the establishment of Opera in Hebrew. There are as yet no theatre buildings in Palestine and the performances have to be given in Cinema Halls adapted for the purpose. A former conductor of Grand Opera in Petrograd and Moscow has come to reside in Palestine, has enlisted singers, has trained his orchestra and chorus, has caused the librettos of several of the classic operas to be translated into Hebrew, and – with the assistance of a few local supporters, but without any subvention – has produced always to crowded houses a series of performances which would do credit to the opera house, if not of the capitals, certainly of the large towns of Europe.

Golinkin's little book also quotes an expression of opinion by the Rt. Hon. Sir Alfred Mond, Bt.:

> I must admit that I went to the Palestine Opera performance without seriously expecting anything accomplished of a high standard. But the artistic acting of the soloists and the lively tenuity of all the members of the troupe have surprised me agreeably. It is difficult to give a just estimation of these performances: they lose a great deal, of course, by the lack of a proper building,

scenery, and suitable inventory. But the acting and singing are by no means commonplace; they are a good deal above average, they approach the standard of first class performances. This institution is highly artistic; and, in my opinion, the Government of Palestine should give it its utmost assistance.

Unfortunately, assistance was not forthcoming, and Mordechai Golinkin's Palestine Opera closed its doors in 1927, its debts being too large to allow it to continue. Golinkin and his wife went on a concert and fundraising tour of the United States. However, upon their return, the Palestine Opera was only able to stage an occasional performance, as, from time to time, did other small opera companies that arose in the Palestine Opera's still smoldering ashes.

Thereafter, the country was to enjoy no further regular opera seasons until 1947, when the American soprano Edis de Philippe founded the Israel National Opera. The early years of that opera company are delightfully described in the autobiography of one of its first singers: Plácido Domingo.[16] But even though Domingo, in his later career, sang in *L'Africaine* and *Le Prophète*, the Israel National Opera never performed Meyerbeer during its entire thirty-one years of active existence. Something had clearly happened to Meyerbeer's reputation since the time of Golinkin, and it happened during the period when European Jewish musicians were fleeing to Palestine.

Those musicians founded the Palestine Symphony Orchestra – later to become the Israel Philharmonic. Paradoxically, Toscanini, who came over as a guest conductor, included excerpts from Wagner's opera *Lohengrin* in his 1937–38 season,[17] but no music by

---

16. Plácido Domingo, *My First Forty Years* (London: Weidenfeld and Nicolson, 1983), 34–42.
17. In their reports of the previous night's concert in Tel Aviv, the April 25 issues of both daily newspapers, *Ha'aretz* and *Yediot Aharonot*, explicitly mention the two *Lohengrin* preludes as having been performed. On the

Meyerbeer. One must understand that this was before Wagner's music came to be associated with the coming Nazi Holocaust. So the paradox is not that *Lohengrin* was in the program. It is rather that this eminent conductor, who had frequently directed performances of Meyerbeer operas[18] in the years before they "went out of fashion," and who was an outspoken anti-fascist and anti-Nazi, might have been expected to include some Meyerbeer in his Palestine concerts. But evidently, the local music-loving public was no longer being encouraged to enjoy this composer.

According to the Israel Philharmonic Orchestra archives, two short Meyerbeer items were included in the programs of 1939, 1942, and 1943. Then, nothing more for nearly half a century, until the 1950 visit of Jan Peerce, whose recital included "O Paradiso" from *L'Africaine*. Once more came another multi-decade gap until 1992, when Luciano Pavarotti sang that same aria. And no further Meyerbeer up to and including the present day.[19] The Wagner effect?

Edis de Philippe died in 1979 and the opera company soon after. There followed a period with no regular opera performances in Israel until, in 1985, the New Israeli Opera came into being. Although they now have an impressive, state-of-the-art opera house and a very respectable repertoire, they too, at the time of this writing, have yet to perform a Meyerbeer opera.

Meyerbeer was, of course, chiefly known for his operas. However, there was a 2003 production in Tel Aviv of *Gli amori di Teolinda*,

---

other hand, a recorded interview with one of the orchestra members, which exists in the Israel radio archive, claims that although the programs had already been printed, Toscanini removed the two Wagner pieces at the last moment as a sign of protest.

18. Harvey Sachs, *Toscanini: Musician of Conscience* (New York: Liveright Publishing, 2017), 21, 29, 31, 35, 45, 49, 58, 122, 124, 176.

19. I wish to thank Ms. Avivit Hochstadter, IPO Archives Manager, for this information.

and some of his smaller-scale works, mostly songs, have appeared in Israel from time to time. Most notably: in 2004, the Kfar Blum Festival included his clarinet quintet with Eli Heifetz, clarinet; and then, in 2013, the same festival dedicated an entire concert to Meyerbeer, featuring the quintet, this time with clarinetist Chen Halevy, but also songs with soprano Sivan Rotem and pianist Jonathan Zak. Of that concert, *Ha'aretz* music critic Noam Ben-Ze'ev wrote enthusiastically:

> *Giacomo Meyerbeer.* From the second third of the nineteenth century for about a hundred years, this name evoked trembling emotions in the West. Meyerbeer – who was the great opera composer, the revolutionary of musical theater, the target of Richard Wagner's envy and anti-Semitic arrows, and the pride of France.
>
> And today? Hardly anybody remembers him. It is true, he is mentioned as the "grand opera" composer, who influenced musical writing in the nineteenth century, but nobody had thought about dedicating a full concert entirely to his works until yesterday afternoon at the Upper Galilee Music Festival in Kfar Blum.
>
> And it was a wonderful concert, well suited for a festival, presenting a familiar personality whose sounds are unfamiliar.
>
> The concert was opened by pianist Jonathan Zak's explanations, with his captivating way of speaking and the deep knowledge of one who delves into the musical scores and their broader historical context, instead of merely looking into Wikipedia in order to prepare himself. He also played throughout most of the program, accompanying soprano Sivan Rotem in songs for voice and piano alone, as well as those with added clarinet and cello.
>
> This was an operatic concert with no opera. Zak contributed drama and color by his orchestral playing – stylistic and pianistic perfection, which was a pleasure to listen to. Sivan Rotem, in

refined and stylistic sensitivity, gave a performance full of charm and beautiful singing. Michal Korman and Chen Halevy, both players in top form, provided further melody, emotion, and personality.

I am not sure how many of the audience hurried out to buy Meyerbeer's operas after this concert, but they certainly did buy Rotem's and Zak's Meyerbeer Songs CD.[20]

Meyerbeer's Clarinet Quintet, with Chen Halevy and a quartet, added a further brilliant operatic dimension to the concert.[21]

Ben-Ze'ev's words "a familiar personality whose sounds are unfamiliar" are a refreshing change from the patronizing tone often adopted by critics who are too embarrassed to admit that they had no idea how wonderful the musical experience could be. Rotem and Zak also performed similar song recitals around the country and issued a second CD in 2016.[22]

It is worth emphasizing that in all of the recent Meyerbeer concerts that were attended by the present author, the audience reaction was extremely positive, and the critics usually indicated how surprised they had been at the quality of this "unknown" music. Why were they surprised? At the occasional revivals of neglected masterpieces by other composers, the critics usually express their delight – but not surprise. In Meyerbeer's case the surprise was that such fine music had lain unknown all their lives. How had this come about? The Wagner effect!

And it is evidently not only music critics whose education too often lacks something. At an illustrated lecture on Meyerbeer given

---

20. *Sivan Rotem, Jonathan Zak: Meyerbeer Songs* (Naxos 8.572367 [one CD]).
21. Noam Ben-Ze'ev, *Ha'aretz*, August 2, 2013; English translation by the present author.
22. *Sivan Rotem, Jonathan Zak, Danny Erdman, Hillel Zori: Meyerbeer Songs, vol. 2* (Naxos 8.573696 [one CD]).

by the present author at an international opera workshop in Jerusalem, among the audience was the director of an important music academy in Eastern Europe. At the end of the lecture, the gentleman stood up and admitted to all present that Meyerbeer had been mentioned, in a course on the history of opera that he had taken as a student, as someone whose music was in bad taste. But no examples had been given, and, as he pointed out, the students obviously had no inclination to seek out for themselves any examples of music by a worthless composer. He emphasized that the musical examples given in the present lecture provided the very first indication for him that Meyerbeer was a great composer.

To be sure, the present author has also experienced negative reactions. For example, a proposal that he and some friends made to the Israel Postal Authority to issue a stamp commemorating the 150th anniversary of Meyerbeer's death, in 2014, was rejected without explanation. It may be presumed that the postal authorities had consulted with some musical experts whom they regarded as being knowledgeable, before arriving at their decision.

In summary then, on the one hand we see that the emphasis by Israel's early settlers on Meyerbeer was as a *Jewish* composer. Later, when musical tastes became dictated by immigrants from Europe, Meyerbeer was out and so too, after the Holocaust, was Wagner. However, at the present time, when controversy is raging in Israel over whether or not to perform operas by Wagner, none by Meyerbeer has been produced for over ninety years, and recitals that include any of his music are still few and far between.

Chapter 15
Finale

This book has made two claims that most readers will have found hard to believe at the start. First, that there was once a world-famous composer whose name and works have been all but forgotten. Second, that this situation came about owing to the deliberate attempt of another famous composer to eradicate his debt to the former. The carefully selected quotations from a wealth of nineteenth-century sources should have sufficed to indicate how extremely celebrated Giacomo Meyerbeer really was as a composer. Hopefully too, the several links that were given to musical examples will have made clear the reason for his erstwhile celebrity, not to mention the enjoyment they may have given to the book's readers.

The book's second claim is probably harder to accept than the first, given the huge reputation of Richard Wagner as a composer. Therefore, before summarizing the evidence, it is important to keep in mind that the world is an infinitely complex place, which we seek to understand from the moment we are born. Comparing the sweet nourishment and warmth we receive from mother with the tasteless and cold floor upon which we first learn to walk, we slowly form an understanding of those parts of the complex world that interact with us directly. At a later stage we go to school where our knowledge of the complex world is enriched by having the learning of others transferred to us. If our instructors are wise, they encourage us always to question received knowledge in order to see how well it fits within our overall understanding. To begin with, when we still understand very little, this process of questioning and fitting is natural and works quite well. However, the older we get, the more complex the world reveals itself to be. As a result, there is a tendency for us to take new information on trust if it comes from what we consider to be a reliable source. But what is a reliable source?

Since this is a book about music and musicians, let us take a look at one sad but documented case of a supposed reliable source. Olin Downes (1886–1955) was a most influential New York music critic during the early part of the twentieth century. In spite of the fact that Gustav Mahler had been hailed by that city's operagoers as one of the greatest opera conductors who had ever graced their shores, and in spite of the fact that some of the then most competent European conductors had occasionally dared to conduct Mahler's enormously complex symphonies in the USA, Downes was prompted to include in his review of the first US performance of Mahler's Fifth Symphony:

> ... Mahler's attempts at solutions, his recoiling before undecipherable enigmas, his gropings and questionings, which in themselves rendered him unable to create symphonies, make him an intensely significant and even imposing figure in music. He attempted things greater than he could do, and failed. His spirit, not his music, commands respect and admiration, ... certainly his music will perish.[1]

In the twenty-first century, with Mahler's symphonies filling concert halls perhaps even more than do Beethoven's, it is hard to believe that a celebrated critic such as Downes could have penned such a

---

1. Olin Downes, *New York Times*, December 3, 1926.

review in one of America's most prestigious newspapers. Perhaps, not surprisingly, Mahler's symphonies were largely neglected in the United States until Leonard Bernstein took up their cause in the 1960s. It is more than likely that the reason for this neglect for so long was due in large measure to the writings of critics such as Downes. Fortunately, in the case of Mahler, music lovers have witnessed a happy ending, and it is perhaps poetic justice that more New Yorkers today know the name Gustav Mahler than that of their city's once eminent music critic. And of course, New York's theater critics have long been infamous for their powers to boost or destroy new plays. Shades of nineteenth-century Paris?

Returning for a moment from the ethereal world of art to the more general issue: the fact is that our lives are simply too complicated for us to find the time always to examine every newly received piece of wisdom before accepting or rejecting it, for to do so, honestly, would require us to reexamine everything we think we know about everything and, if necessary, to remove a piece from that infinite jigsaw puzzle that had been sitting, unknown to us, in the wrong place. Occasionally, if we try hard and are honest enough with ourselves, we can do this. But it is not easy.

In the case of opera, a large part of our present-day received wisdom originated from the writings of Richard Wagner, a man whose ego literally knew no bounds when it came to promoting his own music and his reputation. In so doing, he and his cohorts rode like steamrollers over the reputations of others and did much damage to the development of music in general, not only to opera. The music of late nineteenth-century romantics such as Mendelssohn, Brahms, Bruch, Elgar, and many others was held in contempt as "old-fashioned," with nothing more to offer beyond that which Beethoven had already created. Brahms, alone among the late romantics, managed to survive the Wagnerian onslaught, perhaps because he was the only one who was manifestly "pure German" by

Wagner's standards.² It took another half century for the musical works of these other victims to make their comebacks. Meyerbeer's music is taking longer, for reasons that this book has indicated but which will now be summarized.

There was an initial adoration of Meyerbeer and his operas, for their moral content and the original manner in which they successfully incorporated all of the arts. This is illustrated most clearly in the writings of Giuseppe Mazzini (1805–1872), one of the three leaders of Italy's nineteenth-century independence-from-Austria movement, the so-called Risorgimento. According to Mazzini:

> Meyerbeer is the highest artist of a transition period, in which the High-Priest cannot yet appear. He has given the outline of the musical Drama, and created musical individualities which remind one of Shakespeare. He has inherited from Weber – to whom he owes much – the rare power of reproducing in his music the characteristics of local scenery and manners – witness his truly Breton Pardon de Ploërmel. And he has, as I said, moralized the Drama, making it an echo of the world and its eternal vital problem. He is not a votary of the l'Art pour l'Art music; he is the prophet of the music with a mission, the music standing immediately below Religion.³

The Italian wrote these glowing words in 1867, three years after Meyerbeer's death, and showing a clear appreciation of the Prussian composer's last completed French-language opera. There is not the

---

2. Max Bruch (1838–1920), with supposedly untainted Aryan ancestry (see for example Christoper Fifield, *Max Bruch: His Life and Works* [London: Victor Gollancz, 1988]), was nevertheless regarded with suspicion by the Nazis, possibly because during his lifetime Bruch was widely believed to be a Jew. The English Edward Elgar (1857–1934) was, of course, not even German.
3. Giuseppe Mazzini, letter to Emilie Venturi, May 21, 1867, trans. Marco Pellegrini. Translation used with kind permission of Marco Pellegrini.

slightest hint that Meyerbeer's religion was, for Mazzini, anything but universal.

Unfortunately, as we have seen, at approximately the same time, Richard Wagner was writing:

> Characteristic enough is the attitude adopted by the remaining Jew musicians, nay, by the whole of cultured Jewry, toward their two most renowned composers. To the adherents of Mendelssohn, that famous opera-composer is an atrocity: with a keen sense of honour, they feel how much he compromises Jewdom in the eyes of better trained musicians, and therefore shew no mercy in their judgment.

When Wagner wrote those words, he was subtly working on cultured Jews to turn them against Meyerbeer. As was seen in the chapter on Meyerbeer in Israel, at the start of the twentieth century the Jews of Palestine valued Meyerbeer's music as well as Wagner's. However, by the time Jewish musicians, fleeing to Palestine from Nazi Germany in the 1930s, founded the Palestine Symphony Orchestra (later renamed the Israel Philharmonic), the Wagner poison seemed to be already deeply embedded. Evidence for this is the dearth of Meyerbeer in Israel Philharmonic programs.

The process of Wagnerian indoctrination, not just of Jews, is perhaps nowhere better illustrated than in the writings of Herman Klein (1856–1934). We recall from chapter 11 that in Klein's first meeting with Wagner in London in 1877, he quoted the composer as referring to the need for "agitators" to promote his music. Klein was a prominent British music critic. His fame was based upon the superb writing style of his many newspaper reviews and several books, and on the deep musical erudition he possessed as a voice teacher. These qualities rendered his description of those great singers who lived before the age of reliable sound recordings (e.g., the tenor Jean de Reszke) of lasting value. Here, as an aside, is an example of one such review:

> Of available records from *Les Huguenots* the first to be noticed is the air sung by Raoul in Act I. after the banquet of which he partakes in a mixed company of Catholic and Huguenot nobles. It is a favourite, because of its remarkable combination of poetry and imagination, being the description of a vision of feminine loveliness that Raoul has been privileged to behold. It is a suave and sensuous melody, with a viola obbligato for its well-nigh sole accompaniment; and it is exceedingly difficult to sing. In the Italian version it is known as *Bianca al par di neve alpine*, and the most perfect record of it is that of Enrico Caruso (H.M.V., D.B.115). One artist alone in my experience sang it more ravishingly than Caruso – that was Jean de Reszke; and he never, so far as I am aware, made a record of any sort. But this of the great Italian tenor's is a jewel in every sense of the word – for luscious opulence of tone, for charm of elegant phrasing, for beauty and ease of the big head-notes, for admirable breathing – in short, everything that constitutes a superb artistic vocal effort. It was obviously done when Caruso was just in his prime. More than this there is no need to say.[4]

As may be inferred from this review, Klein was an admirer of Meyerbeer's music. In his *Golden Age of Opera* one finds the following in a description he writes of a London performance of *Les Huguenots* in 1875:

> So there and then it was borne in upon me by an ideal performance that my upbringing had been correct; that my father's taste for Meyerbeer had been founded upon solid grounds; and that the grandeur of this composer's music, which stirred me to my very bones, amply justified the adoration of the generation to which I belonged. Indeed, to have even faintly suggested a

---

4. Herman Klein, "The Gramophone and the Singer: The Treasures of Meyerbeer II," *The Gramophone*, October 1925, reprinted in Letellier, *Reader*, 253.

> doubt of that acknowledged fact would have savoured then either of lunacy or high treason; and I had no particular desire to be thought guilty of either.[5]

By using the word "then" in his closing sentence, Klein was in fact apologizing that in his youth he and everyone else of his generation had loved the music of Meyerbeer but that now (i.e., in 1933 when the book was published) people know better! Interestingly, the 1875 performance of *Les Huguenots* which, at the time, had thrilled Klein, took place a mere two years before he met Wagner. At that time, he could evidently appreciate the greatness of both composers, but by 1933 he, the great and respected music critic, dared no longer admit this!

Golden Age of Opera was actually Klein's third compendium of music criticism. However, neither in his early *Thirty Years of Musical Life in London, 1870–1900* (1903) nor in his *Musicians and Mummers* (1925)[6] can the name Meyerbeer or any of his operas be found in the books' indexes. Verdi and Wagner and a host of other composers and their works are indexed, but not Meyerbeer. And yet both of these books contain copious descriptions of thrilling performances of Meyerbeer operas, but Klein evidently took care that they should not betray, to a casual observer, the author's "treachery." In later life, Klein became a vociferous advocate for a Meyerbeer revival. However, famous as he had been, even in the early part of the century, he had evidently been too frightened back then to swim against the stream – to be thought guilty "either of lunacy or high treason."

Wagner had clearly been at the forefront of this vicious campaign against his former mentor, but Meyerbeer also had some other powerful enemies, both within his profession and on its periphery. As was discussed in chapter 12, his three other most influential

---

5. Herman Klein, *The Golden Age of Opera* (New York: E.P. Dutton, 1933), 33.
6. Herman Klein, *Musicians and Mummers* (London: Cassell, 1925).

enemies were Schumann, with his ill-concealed anti-Semitism, whose severe mental disorder[7] caused him to write many reviews in the form of conversations with his imagined companions "Florestan" or "Eusebius," depending on his mood, and which eventually led him to end his days in a mental institution; Mendelssohn, a devout Protestant, by conversion, who resented being taken for a Jew, even by his fellow Jews, and for whom Meyerbeer represented everything that he wished to leave behind; and Heine, who blackmailed Meyerbeer as an easy source of money.

On the reverse side of the musical controversy were other contemporaries such as Berlioz, Chopin, Liszt, Bizet,[8] etc., who greatly admired Meyerbeer's music, but whose writings sadly lacked the influence that their German counterparts enjoyed. In fact, so penetrating was the anti-Meyerbeer prejudice generated by the German writers that it even distorts the appreciation of French composers by many of today's musicologists.

This can be seen for example in the following quotation taken from the program notes of a CD issued in 1999. The notes are in three languages: German original, and translations into French and English.

> When he composed his *Grand Duo pour piano et violoncelle sur des thèmes de Robert le Diable* in 1832 in collaboration with Franchomme, Chopin was no doubt making concession to fashion because it is hard to imagine Chopin enjoying Meyerbeer's music.[9]

---

7. Ostwald, *Schumann*, 200–201.
8. Bizet, in his grouping of the arts, placed Meyerbeer together with Michelangelo and Beethoven as characterizing "the passionately dramatic," compared with Rossini, Raphael, and Mozart for their "pure and spontaneous" creations. Mina Curtiss, *Bizet and His World* (New York: Alfred A. Knopf, 1958), 72.
9. Ludwik Erhardt, program notes to the CD *Chopin: The 1848 Concert in*

Is it really so hard to imagine Chopin enjoying Meyerbeer's music? They were such close friends that Meyerbeer was a pallbearer at the younger composer's funeral.

Another example of a critic's distortion of evidence is exhibited by a person who is arguably today's foremost expert on Berlioz. After having quoted Berlioz's own words:

> It [*Les Huguenots*] is one of the select circle of masterpieces, along with *Der Freischütz, La Vestale, Fidelio, The Barber of Seville, Don Giovanni* and *Iphigénie en Tauride*, whose performance imposes a respectful silence on the normally talkative musicians...[10]

David Cairns continues, half a page later:

> Once Verdi had absorbed the Meyerbeerian style and re-created it on a higher moral ground, endowing it with much greater melodic invention and dramatic pace, once Wagnerian music-drama had captured the allegiance of the intellectual élite, his eclipse was only a matter of time. Later, when the tidal wave of Wagnerism had receded and the reaction against Romanticism had run its course, Berlioz's music might rise again but not Meyerbeer's....
>
> Yet if we with our superior perspective can "see through" Meyerbeer, few of his contemporaries did....
>
> The admiration of Wagner [in 1841], Verdi, Berlioz and countless other musicians should not really surprise us. The impact of *The Huguenots* and of what Shaw, in the midst of his most impassioned campaigning for Wagner, acknowledged as

---

Paris – Mozart Meyerbeer Bellini Donizetti (Opus 111, OPS 30–263 [one CD]), 12, trans. Peter Hicks.

10. David Cairns, *Berlioz*, vol. 2, *Servitude and Greatness* (Berkeley: University of California Press, 2000), 108–9. Used by permission of University of California Press.

"the electrical Meyerbeerian atmosphere" was understandably enormous....[11]

Just how "we" are supposed to "see through Meyerbeer" is a mystery when, a few sentences later one can read:

> *Robert* created a novel kind of musical dramaturgy. Meyerbeer had devised an operatic theatre which combined all the elements aural and visual – music, words, scenery, costumes, lighting, action, movement – into a coherent whole, and in which the score was at once monumental and fluid, massively constructed and responsive at every moment to the varying demands of the drama; and the process was refined and deepened in *The Huguenots*.[12]

If Cairns were trying to claim that Meyerbeer had composed the most perfect of operas, he could surely not have chosen better words to justify such a claim! So why was he opining that Meyerbeer's music will not "rise again"?

In truth, Berlioz regarded himself as a close friend of Meyerbeer and admired much of his music. However, he was not embarrassed to criticize his friend for those aspects of his operas with which he disagreed (e.g., the great length of the original overture to *Le Prophète*,[13] which Meyerbeer accordingly shortened). After all, that is what friends are for. He also, occasionally, but very occasionally, voiced his jealousy of Meyerbeer's financial ability to snake himself around the corruption of the world of opera in Paris – an ability that many detractors consider a derogatory characteristic of Meyerbeer.

---

11. Cairns, Berlioz, vol. 2, *Servitude and Greatness*, 108–9. Used by permission of University of California Press.
12. Cairns, Berlioz, vol. 2, *Servitude and Greatness*, 108–9. Used by permission of University of California Press.
13. The original overture to *Le Prophète* can be heard on *Giacomo Meyerbeer Overtures and Entr'actes from the French Operas*, New Zealand Symphony Orchestra, cond. Darrell Ang (Naxos 8.573195 [one CD]).

But even if the judgement of Cairns and others of Meyerbeer's *music* could be proven to be true (for example, if there were to exist some concrete criteria by which true art can be judged), it would not account for the subsequent denigration of Meyerbeer's *name*.

That was the contribution of Richard Wagner, who, in the nineteenth century, made a direct appeal to the latent anti-Semitism which, as was illustrated in chapter 12, infected most of his contemporaries. For the majority of opera lovers, who did not study the music in detail, Wagner was such a giant that if he said Meyerbeer's music was trash, then they need look no further into the matter. For those who did know Meyerbeer's music well, such as Klein, it was safer not to swim against the stream by speaking out.

Sadly, this background anti-Semitism seems still to linger on today: for example, in the program notes for a currently available set of CDs of a Meyerbeer opera (to save any unnecessary embarrassment, the source of this quotation will not be identified):

> Some say that he was afraid that Delibes, in his early days as chorus-master at the Opéra, was out to do so [i.e., steal his ideas]. Could it be that, with his sensitive nose, Meyerbeer detected that the future composer of *Coppélia* and *Lakmé* had precisely the gift for spontaneous melody that he lacked?

Let us ignore for the moment the writer's negative judgement on Meyerbeer's gift for inventing melodies; after all, the writer is merely a music critic. Look, instead, on the phraseology he employs for injecting negative thoughts into the composer's mind. Strange, is it not, that the writer should imagine that Meyerbeer would use his nose, rather than his eye or ear, to judge the music of another musician? Would the writer have written the same sentence about Wagner, who, after all, had a nose that was at least as large as Meyerbeer's?

Having thus far presented a case for how Meyerbeer's very name came to be discredited – namely, for basically anti-Semitic reasons – let us look at his legacy.

First, and foremost, it is to be hoped that an unsuspecting reader has discovered some beautiful music, and the place in which it should stand in any honest history of the development of opera. Take, for example, the ballet pieces from act 3 of *Robert le Diable*.[14] Could any of the famous ballets of Tchaikovsky have evolved without such a Meyerbeerian model? Could Verdi's *La Traviata* have taken the form that opera lovers know and love so much had Isabel's act 4 cavatina never been written? Or, could Gounod's *Faust* have sounded as it does without the inspiration of that stirring finale scene in act 5 of *Robert*? These examples all come from a single Meyerbeer opera. His other operas are equally fecund with music that has inspired later composers.

Second, there is a clear moral sub-message in all of Meyerbeer's operas. As a Jew who suffered the stings of religious prejudice all his life, his threefold warning about where religious extremism can lead, as embodied sequentially in *Robert le Diable*, *Les Huguenots*, and *Le Prophète*,[15] is as relevant today as it was during Meyerbeer's lifetime. Even Meyerbeer's dramatic approach to the evils of colonialism, spelled out in *Vasco de Gama* (aka *L'Africaine*), is of prescient significance for the twenty-first century.

By contrast to the moral subtext of Meyerbeer's operas, it is of interest to examine that of Wagner's. It is true *Tannhäuser* is not only about eroticism; that his *Siegfried* is not only about cruelty; and his *Die Meistersinger von Nürnberg* is not only about Teutonic nationalism. These are merely "effects," but as Wagner was fond of emphasizing, his effects (as distinct from Meyerbeer's[16]) all had "causes." And what was that cause? Richard Wagner!

---

14. The ballet pieces from Meyerbeer's operas have all been recorded *on Giacomo Meyerbeer Ballet Music from the Operas*, Barcelona Symphony Orchestra, cond. Michał Nesterowicz (Naxos 8.573076 [1 CD]).
15. Robert Ignatius Letellier, *Religious Themes in French Grand Opéra* (Anif/Salzburg: Verlag Mueller-Speiser, 2009), 17–40.
16. See, for example, Jackson, *Giacomo Meyerbeer: Reputation without Cause?* 157.

But let us leave the last word to composer Camile Saint-Saëns, who, in his perceptive wisdom, wrote:

> Opinions on art – especially on musical art – have at all times been liable to strange aberrations. Art inspires a wealth of suggestion; along this line of thought, chalk can easily be passed off as cheese. The public willingly allows itself to be gulled. On perusing once again what Stendhal said of Cimarosa, what Balzac said of Rossini, one is amazed at the judgments they passed on their contemporaries. The latter listened with gaping mouths,

Composer Camille Saint-Saëns (1835–1921),
who tried to defend the music of Mendelssohn
and Meyerbeer against "the Wagnerites";
photographed 1919 (Wikimedia Commons)

imagining in their simplicity that the reason they did not find in this Italian music everything it was desired to make them see was that they were incapable of understanding it.

Fifty years ago, one dared not express a doubt as to the value of famous Opéras which nowadays it is the fashion to regard as devoid of melody, of harmony, of instrumentation, of everything.... Do not think that I am making up all this; one does not invent such things....

What aberration is it that makes us delight in erroneous reasoning when we can reason correctly, as is possible in the case of those I have mentioned?... In its essence, art does not change; men only change their minds as to its methods and limitations. Once they become certain that these latter are purely arbitrary and that everything in the realm of the beautiful has a right to live, they will more easily conceive of the inexhaustible fecundity of art.[17]

So, in order to clear the air, let us, along with Saint-Saëns, accept what is beautiful as beautiful, and not worry about whether it conforms to any given opinion about what art should be. Opinions follow fashion, but art is eternal. Like the poet's Grecian urn, one may say of Meyerbeer's music:

> *When old age shall this generation waste,*
> *Thou shalt remain, in midst of other woe*
> *Than ours, a friend to man, to whom thou say'st,*
> *"Beauty is truth, truth beauty – that is all*
> *Ye know on earth, and all ye need to know."*[18]

---

17. Cited in Studd, *Saint-Saëns*, 302–4.
18. John Keats, "Ode on a Grecian Urn," in *The Oxford Book of English Verse, 1250–1918*, ed. Sir Arthur Quiller-Couch (Oxford: Oxford University Press, 1955), 745–74.

Appendix 1

Early Meyerbeer Recordings

Meyerbeer's work was first performed well before there was such a thing as sound recording (the first-ever sound recording took place in 1860). By the beginning of the twentieth century, however, at the dawn of sound recording, there were multiple recorded operatic examples of his work. The following four tables list the five most-recorded numbers from Meyerbeer's grand operas, together with the number of artists known to have recorded them. The statistics have been compiled from data given in the Meyerbeer discography by Arsenty and Letellier. CD reissues of recordings of any given singer from that era will usually contain one or two Meyerbeer arias. However, two all-Meyerbeer compilations are particularly worthy of mention: two three-CD collections entitled *Meyerbeer on Record*, on Marston Records (www.marstonrecords.com); and five individual CDs, one for each of the grand operas, and one for the two opéras-comiques, from Paradise Records (jstephens34@austin.rr.com).

Table 1: The five most recorded arias from *Robert le Diable* at the start of the twentieth century

Rank	Aria	Character	No. of artists who recorded it
1	Act 3 : Voici donc les débris … Nonnes qui reposez	Bertram, bass	49
2	Act 4 : Robert, Robert, toi que j'aime	Isabel, soprano	37
3	Act 3 : Encore un de gagné ! … Noirs démons, fantômes	Bertram, bass	10
4	Act 1 : Va, dit-elle, va, mon enfant	Alice, soprano	8
5	Act 1 : O fortune, à ton caprice	Robert, tenor	8

Table 2: The five most recorded arias from *Les Huguenots* at the start of the twentieth century

Rank	Aria	Character	No. of artists who recorded it
1	Act 1 : Plus blanche que la blanche hermine	Raoul, tenor	107
2	Act 1: Nobles seigneurs salut!	Urbain, contralto	98
3	Act 1: Piff, paff, piff, paff!	Marcel, bass	63
4	Act 2 : O beau pays de la Touraine	Marguerite, soprano	52
5	Act 1 : Seigneur, rempart et seul soutien	Marcel, bass	40

Table 3: The five most recorded pieces from *Le Prophète* at the start of the twentieth century

Rank	Aria	Character	No. of artists who recorded it
1	Act 2 : Ah, mon fils, sois béni !	Fidès, contralto	57
2	Act 4: Marche du sacre (Coronation march)	Orchestra	41
3	Act 3 : Roi du ciel et des anges	Jean, tenor	29
3	Act 2 : Pour Berthe, moi je soupire	Jean, tenor	29
5	Act 4 : Donnez, donnez pour une pauvre âme	Fidès, contralto	22

Table 4: The five most recorded arias from *L'Africaine* at the start of the twentieth century

Rank	Aria	Character	No. of artists who recorded it
1	Act 4 : O paradis sorti de l'onde	Vasco de Gama, tenor	204
2	Act 2 : Fille des rois, à toi l'hommage	Nélusko, bass	75
3	Act 3 : Adamastor, roi des vagues profondes	Nélusko, bass	68
4	Act 2 : Sur mes genoux, fils du soleil	Sélika, soprano	34
5	Act 4 : L'avoir tant adorée	Nélusko, bass	23

Appendix 2
Palestine Opera Productions

First-night details of the seventeen productions of the short-lived Palestine Opera from 1923 to 1927[1]

Opera	Composer	Translator	Premiere	City
La Traviata	Verdi	A. Aschmann	July 28, 1923*	Tel Aviv
Rigoletto	Verdi	M. Freidmann	October 30, 1923	Jerusalem
Pagliacci	Leoncavallo	M. Freidmann	January 9, 1924	Tel Aviv
Faust	Gounod	A. Aschmann	February 19, 1924	Jerusalem
Romeo et Juliette	Gounod	A. Aschmann	April 14, 1924	Jerusalem
La Juive	Halévy	M. Freidmann	June 17, 1924	Jerusalem
Aida	Verdi	A. Schlonsky	November 20, 1924	Tel Aviv
Il Trovatore	Verdi	A. Aschmann	December 21, 1924	Jerusalem
Tosca	Puccini	M. Freidmann	January 22, 1925	Tel Aviv
Samson et Dalila	Saint-Saëns	A. Aschmann	March 12, 1925	Tel Aviv
Otello	Verdi	Y. Dushmann	April 27, 1925	Jerusalem
Cavaleria Rusticana	Mascagni	M. Freidmann	June ?, 1925	Tel Aviv

---

1. Alfred Loewenberg, *Annals of Opera, 1597–1940* (Cambridge, UK: W. Heffer and Sons, 1943).

Opera	Composer	Translator	Premiere	City
Carmen	Bizet	A. Aschmann	November 10, 1925	Tel Aviv
Die Maccabäer	Anton Rubinstein	M. Freidmann	December 15, 1925	Jerusalem
Rusalka	Dargo-Muizhsky	A. Aschmann	May 3, 1926	Jerusalem
Les Huguenots	Meyerbeer	A. Aschmann	December 12, 1926**	Jerusalem
Il barbiere di Siviglia	Rossini	M. Freidmann	February 23, 1927	Jerusalem

* July 26, 1923, according to Hirschberg
** December 9, 1926, in Tel Aviv, according to newspaper advertisements

An Annotated Bibliography

Arsenty, Richard, and **Robert Ignatius Letellier.** *Giacomo Meyerber: The Complete Libretti in Five Volumes.* Newcastle upon Tyne: Cambridge Scholars Publishing, 2004. The librettos of all Meyerbeer operas are given, each in its original language – French, German, or Italian, as the case may be – and in English translation. Although some of the (often heavily cut) recordings include a libretto, those in these volumes are more complete.

———. *Giacomo Meyerbeer: A Discography of Vintage Recordings, 1889–1955.* Newcastle upon Tyne: Cambridge Scholars Publishing, 2013. An indispensable compilation of all known recordings: artists, labels, year, matrix number, etc. No music lover, interested in singers from the early years of sound recording, should be without it.

Becker, Heinz, and Gudrun Becker. *Giacomo Meyerbeer: A Life in Letters.* Translated by Mark Violette. Portland, OR: Amadeus Press, 1983. Perhaps nothing tells us more about a composer's character than the letters he writes. This volume contains a selection of exchanges between Meyerbeer, his family, his friends, his fellow composers, and others, yielding a deep insight into his character and personality.

Blumenthal, W. Michael. *The Invisible Wall: Germans and Jews.* Washington, DC: Counterpoint, 1998. This is a fascinating history about the author's own family, which included among its numbers many famous intellectuals – including Meyerbeer – dating back to the period when Jews first settled in Prussia. The book sheds much light upon the futile attempts of successive generations of German Jews – up to Blumenthal's own father – to gain social acceptance in their homeland.

Everist, Mark. *Giacomo Meyerbeer and Music Drama in Nineteenth-Century Paris*. Aldershot, UK: Ashgate Variorum, 2005. This collection of the author's essays includes important studies on: *La nymphe du Danube* (a pastiche, which Meyerbeer was commissioned to write, using music culled from his Italian operas, but which he had to abandon); the Italian operas *Margherita d'Anjou* and *Il crociato in Egitto*; the origins of the grand opera *Robert le Diable*; and Meyerbeer's two opéras comiques.

———. *Music Drama at the Paris Odéon, 1824–1828*. Berkeley: University of California Press, 2002. This is a most valuable study, by one of the foremost Meyerbeer specialists, of the musico-political structure of Paris during the period in which Giacomo Meyerbeer first began working in that city.

Gerhard, Anselm. *The Urbanization of Opera: Music Theater in Paris in the Nineteenth Century*. Translated by Mary Whittall. Chicago: University of Chicago Press, 1998. This book, which is heavily dominated by the role of Meyerbeer, contains important studies of *Les Huguenots* and *Le Prophète*, and of grand operas by some of his contemporaries.

Golinkin, Mordechai. *Mi-Heichalei Yefet l'Ohalei Shem*. Translated from Russian to Hebrew by Yaakov Adini. Tel Aviv: privately published, 1957. An autobiography of the conductor who founded the Palestine Opera in 1923 and produced *Les Huguenots* in 1926–27.

HaCohen, Ruth. *The Music Libel against the Jews*. New Haven: Yale University Press, 2011. This fascinating book traces the history of the manner in which music has served as an instrument for anti-Semitism. It includes extremely original comparative analyses of Meyerbeer's *Le Prophète*, George Eliot's *Daniel Deronda*, and Wagner's *Parsifal*.

Jackson, Jennifer. *Giacomo Meyerbeer: Reputation without Cause? A Composer and His Critics.* Newcastle upon Tyne, UK: Cambridge Scholars Publishing, 2011. This thoroughly researched and well-written book presents the history of each of Meyerbeer's operas, together with what their contemporary newspapers wrote – both positive and negative. She ponders the reasons that so much effort was made to denigrate him if he was really as worthless a composer as his detractors claimed.

Kelly, Thomas Forrest. *First Nights at the Opera.* New Haven: Yale University Press, 2004. This delightful coffee-table book documents in wonderful detail the premiere performances of five great operas: Handel's *Giulio Cesare*; Mozart's *Don Giovanni*, Meyerbeer's *Les Huguenots*, Wagner's *Das Rheingold*, and Verdi's *Otello*. For each first night, the author provides a cornucopia of pictorial material relevant to the venue and period, the social and political background, a description of the plot and of the singers, newspaper reviews, and much else.

Klein, Herman. *The Golden Age of Opera.* New York: E.P. Dutton, 1933. This is an equally enjoyable follow-up to the earlier book (below). By this time, however, Klein had become such a well-respected music critic that he evidently no longer feared placing Meyerbeer's name and works in the book's index.

———. *Thirty Years of Musical Life in London, 1870–1900.* New York: The Century Company, 1903. This book provides eloquent, contemporary descriptions of great Meyerbeer vocal performances, many by singers who lived before the recording era and who therefore left no other tangible mementos. Klein (1856–1934) was a voice teacher and a gifted writer who, more than many others, enables us to peer into this otherwise forgotten age. Interestingly enough, although the book contains copious positive descriptions of great Meyerbeer performances, unlike those of all other composers, Meyerbeer's name does not appear in its index!

Köhler, Joachim. *Richard Wagner: The Last of the Titans.* Translated by Stewart Spencer. (New Haven: Yale University Press, 2004). This highly readable psychological study of Wagner and each of his operas sheds important light on his attitude toward Meyerbeer.

Letellier, Robert Ignatius, trans. and ed. *The Diaries of Giacomo Meyerbeer.* 4 vols. Cranbury, NJ: Associated University Presses, 1999, 2001, 2002, 2004. No words can praise these volumes too highly. All references of Meyerbeer to other people, art works, plays, musical compositions, political events, etc., have been meticulously researched and are carefully explained in extensive footnotes collected at the end of each year's diary entries. The fourth volume details all of Meyerbeer's known compositions – published, unpublished, and uncompleted – and where their manuscripts may (where known) be found. It also provides an extensive list of compositions that other composers (such as Liszt, Johann Strauss, father and son, etc.) based on Meyerbeer's operas. Each volume is indexed, making it easy to find issues of interest.

———. *Giacomo Meyerbeer: A Critical Life and Iconography.* Newcastle upon Tyne, UK: Cambridge Scholars Publishing, 2018. A detailed study of Meyerbeer's life, his work, his surroundings, those with whom he came into contact, and much more. The ideal follow-up for any reader of the present book who wishes to learn in greater depth about this remarkable composer.

———. *Giacomo Meyerbeer: A Reader.* Newcastle upon Tyne: Cambridge Scholars Publishing, 2007. A fascinating collection of reprinted articles about Meyerbeer, by a variety of writers who date from the composer's own time until the present.

———. *Meyerbeer Studies: A Series of Lectures, Essays, and Articles on the Life and Work of Giacomo Meyerbeer.* Madison, WI: Fairleigh Dickinson University Press, 2005. This is a highly readable and informative collection of essays and articles by the author on the life and works of Meyerbeer.

———. *The Operas of Giacomo Meyerbeer.* Cranbury, NJ: Associated University Presses, 2006). A detailed discussion of all of Meyerbeer's operas. Extremely useful pre-reading before attending one of them for the first time.

Rosenthal, Harold, ed. *The Mapleson Memoirs: The Career of an Operatic Impressario, 1858–1888.* London: Putnam, 1966. This book depicts the career of the operatic impresario James Henry Mapleson (1830–1901) during the years 1858 to 1888. Meyerbeer was, not surprisingly, a staple part of Mapleson's repertoire, and the comic and tragic events that accompanied the traveling career of his troupe make for fascinating reading.

Sposato, Jeffrey S. *The Price of Assimilation: Felix Mendelssohn and the Nineteenth-Century Anti-Semitic Tradition.* Oxford: Oxford University Press, 2006. This book is an important recent study of Mendelssohn and his choral music. It makes no explicit reference to Meyerbeer, but it emphasizes the kind of prejudices with which both composers had to deal, and helps us, perhaps, to understand something of the antipathy the two composers felt toward each other.

Index

A

Abbey, Henry E. (1846–1896, manager of New York Metropolitan Opera), 144
L'Académie-Royal de Musique, Paris (L'Opéra), 50, 55
Arsenty, Richard (1945–2013, American translator of opera libretti), 117
Auber, Daniel (1782–1871, French composer), 10, 58
    Gustave III, 58
    La Muette de Portici, 58

B

Bach, Johann Sebastian (1685–1750, German composer), 174
Bacher, Joseph (Dr. of Jurisprudence), 126
Baermann, Heinrich Joseph (1784–1847, German clarinet virtuoso), 29
Balf, Michael William (1808–1870, Irish composer), 71
Balfour Declaration, 187
Balzac, Honoré de (1799–1850, French writer), 54, 214
Barbier, Jules (1825–1901, French librettist), 86
St. Bartholomew's Night massacre, 60, 103
Bauernfeld, Eduard von (1802–1890, Austrian dramatist), 126
Beer, Amalia née Malka Wulff (1767–1854, Meyerbeer's mother), 14, 15, 17
Beer, Heinrich (1794–1842, Meyerbeer's brother), 14, 20
Beer, Jakob, originally Juda Herz (1769–1825, Meyerbeer's father), 14
Beer, Liebmann Meyer (Meyerbeer's childhood name), 13–24
Beer, Michael (1800–1833, Meyerbeer's playwright brother), 14, 72
Beer, Wilhelm (1797–1850, Meyerbeer's astronomer brother), 14
Beethoven, Ludwig van (1770–1827, German composer), 10, 27, 151, 154, 165, 169, 174, 175, 186, 203, 204, 209n8

Fidelio, opera in 2 acts, op. 72, 25, 26, 34, 155–56, 156, 159, 160, 210

Leonora, first version of *Fidelio*, in 3 acts, 22

Symphony no. 7 in A Major, op. 92, 26

Bellaigue, Camile (1858–1930, French music critic), 139–40

Bellini, Vincenzo (1801–1835, Italian composer), 40, 86, 160

Norma, 79, 146

I Puritani, 86, 142

La Sonnambula, 36, 142

Ben-Ze'ev, Noam (Israeli music critic), 200

Berlioz, Hector (1803–1869, French composer and music critic), 61–64, 87, 95, 156, 158, 209, 210–11

Bernstein, Leonard (1918–1990, American composer and conductor), 204

Bible

Esther, 179

Judges, 23

Psalm 134, 21

Birch-Pfeiffer, Charlotte (1800–1868, German actress and writer), 129

Bizet, Georges (1838–1875, French composer), 209, 209n8

Carmen, 142

Blaze, François-Henri-Joseph, aka Castil-Blaze (1784–1857, French music critic), 47

Boeticher, Louis (1813–1867, German operatic bass), 157

Boito, Arrigo (1842–1918, Italian composer, librettist for Verdi), 142

Mefistofele, 142

Borg, Alexander (Maltese linguist), 166n1

Borrel, Alfred (1836–1927, French medal maker), 37, 38

Brahms, Johannes (1833–1897, German composer), 168, 174, 204

Bruch, Max (1838–1920, German composer), 204, 205n2

Bülow, Cosima von, née Liszt (1837–1930, wife of Hans von Bülow, later wife of Richard Wagner), 166, 175, 181

Bülow, Hans von (1830–1894, German conductor), 181

Burguis, Mr. (secretary to Meyerbeer's mother), 149

Busoni, Ferruccio (1866–1924, Italian pianist and composer), 77

Byron, Lord George Gordon (1788–1824, English poet), 60

C

Cairns, David (British musicologist), 210–11, 212

Carré, Michel (1822–1872, French librettist), 86

Caruso, Enrico (1873–1921, Italian operatic tenor), 2, 207

INDEX

Charles x (king of France, 1824–1830), 51
Chaliapin, Feodor (1873–1938, Russian operatic bass), 190
Chopin, Frédéric (1810–1849, Polish pianist and composer), 52, 71, 119, 151–53, 154, 159, 165, 169, 209, 210
    Ballade no. 2 in F Major, op. 38, 52n10
    Duo concertant in E Major, 52, 153, 209
Cimarosa, Domenico (1749–1801, Italian composer), 214
Clementi, Muzio (1752–1832, Italian composer), 17
Conan Doyle, Arthur (1859–1930, British novelist), 64
Congress of Vienna, 26–27, 51
Corbould, Edward (1814–1905, British artist), 79
Costa, Michael (1808–1884, British-Italian conductor), 85–86
Court Theater, Stuttgart, 25

D

da Gama, Vasco (c. 1464–1524, Portuguese explorer), 80, 108
Degas, Edgar (1834–1917, French artist), 56, 56n16
Delavigne, Germain (1790–1868, French librettist), 48, 51
Delibes, Léo (1836–1891, French composer), 212
    Coppélia, 212
    Lakmé, 212
de Reszke, Édouard (1853–1917, operatic bass), 2, 66, 145
de Reszke, Jean (1850–1925, operatic tenor), 2, 65, 145, 206–7
de Soto, Hernando (c. 1496–1542, Spanish explorer), 80
di Bassetto, Corno. *See* George Bernard Shaw
Dieren, Bernard van (1887–1936, Dutch composer), 8n5
Domingo, Plácido (Spanish operatic tenor), 111, 197
Donizetti, Gaetano (1797–1848, Italian composer), 119
    Lucia di Lammermoor, 79, 142, 146
d'Ortigue, Joseph (1802–1866, French philosopher), 181
Downes, Olin (1886–1955, American music critic), 203–4
Dumas (père), Alexandre (1802–1870, French writer), 54–55
Duponchel, Henri (1794–1868, managing director of Paris Opéra), 74

E

Eden Cinema, Jaffa, 191
Edward vii (king of UK, 1901–1910), 2
Elgar, Edward (1857–1934, English composer), 204, 205n2
Everist, Mark (British musicologist), 8n4, 46n4, 47n6, 49, 81n1

F

Fiorentino, Pier Angelo (1811–1864, Italian journalist), 135
Flotow, Friedrich von (1812–1833, German composer), 142
  Martha, 142
Fontana, Juljan (1810–1869, Polish pianist), 151–53
Franchomme, August-Joseph (1808–1884, French cellist and composer), 209
Franconi, Antonio (1737–1836, Italian circus impresario), 156
Frederick the Great (king of Prussia, 1740–1786), 73, 81, 82
Frederick William II (king of Prussia, 1786–1797), 11
Friedrich Wilhelm III (king of Prussia, 1797–1840), 15, 26
Friedrich Wilhelm IV (king of Prussia, 1840–1861), 18, 71, 119
Freigedank, K. (alias of Richard Wagner), 170

G

Gaebler, Regierungsrat (German councilor), 126
Gänsbacher, Johann Baptist (1778–1844, Austrian composer), 21
Gilbert, William Schwenck (1836–1911, English dramatist and librettist), 57
Gluck, Christoph Willibald (1714–1787, German composer), 54, 69
  Armide, 62
  Iphigénie en Tauride, 210
Golinkin, L. (operatic soprano, first wife of Mordechai Golinkin), 195n14
Golinkin, Miriam (operatic soprano, second wife of Mordechai Golinkin), 197
Golinkin, Mordechai (1875–1963, Russian-born conductor), 189–97
Goryainov, Matvey (operatic bass), 194
Gounod, Charles-François (1818–1893, French composer), 142, 144
  Faust, 79, 86, 87, 142, 192, 213
  Romeo et Juliette, 144
Gradenwitz, Peter (1910–2001, Israeli musicologist), 190n11
Grattenauer, Karl Wilhelm Friedrich (1773–1838, German anti-Semitic pamphleteer), 17
Grimm, The Brothers (Jacob Ludwig Karl, 1785–1863 and Wilhelm Carl, 1786–1859), 150, 168
Grüneisen, Charles (1806–1879, English journalist and music critic), 41

H

Habeneck, François-Antoine (1781–1849, French violinist and conductor), 61, 64
HaCohen, Ruth (Israeli musicologist), 160–61

INDEX

Hähnel, Amalie (1807–1849, Austrian operatic mezzo-soprano), 40
Halevy, Chen (Israeli clarinetist), 199–200
Halévy, Fromental (1799–1862 French composer)
La Juive, 58
Handel, Georg Frideric (1865–1759, German composer), 69
Hanslick, Eduard (1825–1904, German music critic), 73–75
Harlas, Hélène (1775–1818, German operatic soprano), 29
Harmonischer Verein, Der, 21
Heifetz, Eli (Israeli clarinetist), 199
Heine, Carl (uncle of Heinrich Heine), 124
Heine, Heinrich (1797–1856, German poet), 55, 58, 60, 77–78, 119, 122, 124–25, 132–33, 139, 148, 165n22, 209
Henderson, William James (1855–1937, American music critic), 144–45, 146
Hérold, Louis-Ferdinand (1791–1833, French operatic composer), 10, 160
Ferdinand Hiller (1811–1885, German composer), 164
Hirshberg, Jehoash (Israeli musicologist), 186
Hochstadter, Avivit (Israeli music archivist), 198n19
Hofmeister, Friedrich (1782–1864, Leipzig music publisher), 151
Hofoper Theater, Munich, 24
Humboldt, Alexander von (1769–1859, Prussian explorer), 18

I

Israel National Opera, 197
Israeli Opera, 198
Israel Philharmonic Orchestra, 197, 198, 206
Istel, Edgar (1880–1948, German composer and musicologist), 24

J

Jackson, Jennifer (British musicologist), 37, 37n9
Jewish State, The (Herzl), 185
John of Leyden (1509–1536, Dutch Anabaptist leader), 76
July Revolution, 51
Jurowski, Michail (Russian conductor), 114

K

Kärntnertor Theater, Vienna, 25
Kaskel, Baron Karl, (1797–1874, banker, husband of Victoire), 129
Kaskel, Madam Victoire née Fränkel (1811–1843), 117, 127n19
Kastner, Jean-Georges (1810–1867, French composer), 37
Keats, John (1795–1821, English poet), 25
Klein, Herman(n) (1856–1934, English voice teacher and music critic), 8n5, 140, 206–8, 212

Köhler, Joachim (German music critic), 166, 181–82n15
Korman, Michal (Israeli cellist), 200
Krehbiel, Henry (1854–1923, American musicologist and critic), 144
Kurpinski, Karol (1785–1857, Polish composer)
The Charlatan, 52n8

L

Lambert, Constant (1905–1951, British composer), 76
Lasserre, Pierre (1867–1930, French critic), 137–39, 146
Lauska, Ignace (1769–1821, Moravian pianist), 15, 19
Letellier, Robert Ignatius (British musicologist), 23–24, 24–25n7, 31, 39, 52n10, 117, 118, 127, 127n19, 165n22, 194n13
Leoncavallo, Ruggero (1857–1919, Italian composer)
I Pagliacci, 192
Levasseur, Nicolas-Prosper (1791–1871, French operatic bass), 55
Levin, Jente Enoch (d. 1808, Meyerbeer's paternal grandmother), 11n2
Lilienblum, Moshe Leib (1843–1910, Zionist leader), 185–86
Lind, Jenny (1820–1887, Swedish operatic soprano), 2, 73, 82, 164

Liszt, Franz (1811–1886, Hungarian composer and virtuoso pianist), 76–77, 161, 161–62n16, 209
Ad nos, ad salutarem undam for organ, S.259, 76
Reminiscences of Robert le Diable, S.413, 53
Louis XVIII (king of France, 1814–1824), 25n8, 51
Louis Philippe (king of France, 1830–1848), 51
Ludwig I (king of Bavaria, 1825–1848), 14n7
Ludwig II (king of Bavaria, 1864–1886), 180, 181–82n15
Lüttichau, August Freiherr von (1786–1863, director of Dresden theaters), 122

M

Mädler, Johann Heinrich (1794–1874, German astronomer), 14n6
Mahler, Gustav (1860–1911, Austro-Bohemian composer), 129, 203–4
Die drei Pintos, 129
Symphony no. 5 in C Minor, 203
Malibran, Maria Felicia (1808–1836, Spanish operatic soprano and contralto), 41
Maurel, Victor (1848–1923, French operatic baritone), 145
Mazzini, Giuseppe (1805–1872, Italian politician), 205–6, 205n2

Melba, Nellie (1861–1931, Australian operatic soprano), 2, 145
Mendelssohn, Felix (1809–1847, German composer), 1, 14n5, 133–35, 141, 153–54, 161, 164, 165n22, 170, 173–79, 182, 183, 186, 204, 206, 209
  Elias, op. 70, 134
  Piano concerto no. 2 in D Minor, op. 40, 53
  Symphony no. 5 in D Major/Minor, op. 107 ("Reformation"), 181
Mendelssohn, Moses (1729–1786, German-Jewish philosopher, grandfather of Felix), 164
Metastasio, Pietro (1698–1782, Italian poet and librettist), 31
Metropolitan Opera, New York, 141–46
Meyer, Rebecca (1793–1850, wife of Meyerbeer's brother Heinrich), 14n5
Meyerbeer, Alfred (1828–1829, only son of Meyerbeer, died in infancy), 50, 121
Meyerbeer, Blanca (1830–1896, daughter of Meyerbeer), 50, 70, 120, 131–32
Meyerbeer, Caecilie (1837–1931, daughter of Meyerbeer), 70
Meyerbeer, Cornelie (1842–1922, daughter of Meyerbeer), 70, 121
Meyerbeer, Eugenie (1827–1827, first daughter of Meyerbeer, died in infancy), 49, 121

Meyerbeer, Giacomo
  L'Africaine, 70, 71, 79–80, 88, 89, 97, 108–11, 117, 139, 194, 197, 198, 213
  Alimelek, oder Die beiden Kalifen, 25–27, 34, 38
  Alamanzor, 37–38
  "Aspiration," 131n29
  Gli amori di Teolinda, 29, 198
  "An Victoire, am Rhein," 127n19
  "Ariette," 21n3
  Das Brandenburger Tor, 26n8, 38, 39
  "Canzonette," 21n3
  choral pieces, 72, 118, 131n30
  "Coronation March," 76
  Il Crociato in Egitto, 38, 39–41, 43–45, 46, 50, 52, 118, 156
  Dinorah, 86–87, 92, 114–17, 143, 185
  Emma di Resburgo, 33–35, 38, 46
  L'Esule di Granata, 36–39
  L'Étoile du Nord, 38, 73, 76, 81, 83–85, 86, 87, 112–14, 143
  Ein Feldlager in Schlesien, 71–75, 81–82
  Der Fischer und das Milchmädchen, 19
  Gott und die Natur, 21
  "Hallelujah," 131n28
  "Hör ich das Liedchen klingen," 124n12
  Les Huguenots, 2, 38, 58, 60–69, 70–71, 73, 75, 76, 79, 87, 88, 102–6, 111, 117, 121, 139, 141–42, 144–45, 146, 155–61, 165, 193–95, 207–8, 210–11, 213

Italian songs, 21
Jephtas Gelübde, 23–25, 29, 38
"Klopstock Lieder," 131n30
"Komm, du schönes Fischermädchen," 124n12
Margherita d'Anjou, 35–36, 38, 40, 45–46, 118
Marguerite d'Anjou, 46
"Menschenfeindlich," 14n7
"Mina," 14n7
La Nymphe du Danube, 46–47
Le Pardon de Ploërmel, 86–87, 88, 114–17, 205
Les Patineurs, 76
Le Prophète, 38, 70, 71, 74–80, 87, 92, 106–8, 117, 121, 139, 141, 142, 197, 211, 213
Psalm 134, 21
Romilda e Costanza, 30–31, 33, 38, 39, 47
"Die Rose, die Lilie, die Taube, die Sonne," 124n12
"Scholar's fugue," 19
"Scirocco," 14n7
Semiramide riconosciuta, 31–33, 38
Struensee, 14n7, 71
torch dances, 72
"Uvnucho Yomar," 131n27
Vasco de Gama, 80, 88, 89, 97, 108, 110, 111, 214
Vielka, 73, 82
Wirt und Gast, oder Aus Scherz Ernst, 25, 34
Meyerbeer, Minna née Mosson (1804–1886, married Meyerbeer in 1826), 45n2, 46, 50, 70, 120, 121, 128

Mond, Sir Alfred (1868–1930, industrialist, financier, politician, Zionist), 196
Mosson, Minna. *See* Meyerbeer, Minna
Mozart, Wolfgang Amadeus (1756–1791, Austrian composer), 10, 16, 17, 20, 22, 27, 160, 174, 186, 209n8
  Cosi fan tutte, 159
  Don Giovanni, 68, 77n5, 79, 100, 142, 144, 159
  Don Juan. *See* Mozart: *Don Giovanni*
  Magic Flute, The. *See* Mozart: *Die Zauberflöte*
  Le Nozze di Figaro, 77n5, 159
  Symphony no. 40 in G Minor, 99
  Die Zauberflöte, 68

N

Napoleon Bonaparte (1769–1821), 25
Nejedlý, Karel (1873–1927, Czech artist), 69
Nietzsche, Friedrich (1844–1900, German philosopher), 167, 168, 172, 180
Nordau, Max (1849–1923, Hungarian physician, Zionist leader), 167
Nordica, Lillian (1857–1914, American operatic soprano), 145

O

Offenbach, Jacques (1819–1889, German-French composer), 81

Olivier, Émile (1825–1913, French statesman), 9

P

Paganini, Niccolò (1782–1840, Italian violin virtuoso and composer), 36

Palestine Opera, 191–97

Palestine Symphony Orchestra (later Israel Philharmonic Orchestra), 197, 206

Pavarotti, Luciano (Spanish operatic tenor), 198

Peerce, Jan (1904–1984, American operatic tenor), 198

Pellegrini, Marco Clemente (Italian musicologist), 205n3

Philippe, Edis de (1912–1979, American-Israeli operatic soprano), 197

Picasso, Pablo (1881–1973, Spanish artist), 167

Pillet, Léon-François-Raymond (1803–1868, director of Paris Opéra), 70–71, 74

Pixérécourt, Guilbert-René-Charles de (1773–1844, French playwright, director of Paris Opéra-Comique), 36, 46, 48, 49

Plançon, Pol (1851–1914, French operatic bass), 145

Pleyel, Ignaz Joseph (1757–1831, Austrian-French composer and piano builder), 151–52

Ponchielli, Amilcare (1834–1886, Italian composer)
  La Gioconda, 142

Probst, Heinrich Albert (1791–1846, Leipzig music publisher, Paris agent), 151–52

Prussian Academy of Arts, 17

R

Radecke, Robert (1830–1911, German composer and conductor), 163

Redern, Friedrich Wilhelm von (1802–1883, Prussian nobleman, director of royal court music), 123

Reid, Donald M. (American historian), 187n6

Richter, Hans (1843–1916, Austrian-Hungarian conductor), 140

Ries, Ferdinand (1784–1838, German composer), 155

Rishon leZion orchestra, 185, 186

Romani, Felice (1788–1865, Italian poet and librettist), 35–36, 46

Roqueplan, Louis-Victor (1805–1870, codirector Paris Opéra 1847–1854, director Opéra-Comique 1857–1860), 74

Rosenthal, Harold (1917–1987, English music critic), 84

Rossi, Gaetano (1774–1855, Italian opera librettist), 30, 32, 33, 34, 37

Rossini, Gioacchino (1792–1868, Italian composer), 30, 43, 91, 93, 94, 95n7, 160, 209n8, 214
  Il barbiere di Siviglia, 142, 146, 193
  Edoardo e Cristina, 35
  Guillaume Tell, 79
  Ivanhoé, 47–48
  "Quelques mesures de chant funèbre à mon pauvre ami Meyerbeer 8 heures du matin – Paris 6 mai 1864," 93
  Semiramide, 33, 33n4, 43
  Il viaggio a Reims, 43
Rotem, Sivan (Israeli operatic soprano), 199–200
Rojansky, Arnon (1900–1966, operatic tenor), 194
Rubinstein, Anton Grigoryevich (1829–1894, Russian composer), 193
  Die Maccabäer, 193
Ruppin, Shulamith (1873–1912, German-Palestinian music pedagogue), 186, 191
Royal Albert Hall, London, 140
Royal Festival Hall, London, 36
Royal Italian Opera, Covent Garden, London, 84–86
Royal Theater, Dresden, 123

S

Saint-Saëns, Camille (1835–1921, French composer), 141, 214–15
  Samson et Dalila, 193
Salieri, Antonio (1750–1825, Italian composer), 27, 28, 29, 31, 73
Salle Favart, Paris, 43, 44
Salle Louvois, Paris, 43, 46
Salvi, Dario (Anglo-Italian musicologist and conductor), 25, 27, 27n14, 31
Samuel, Sir Herbert (1870–1963, High Commissioner for Palestine), 196
Sauvage, Thomas-Maria-François (1794–1877, French dramatist), 46
Sayn-Wittgenstein, Princess Carolyne (1819–1887, Polish noblewoman, writer), 161–62n16
Scalchi, Sofia (1850–1922, Italian operatic contralto and mezzo-soprano), 145
Schlesinger, Maurice (1798–1871, Paris music publisher), 151–52
Schlüter, Dr. Joseph (German music historian), 149
Schmidt-Hensel, Roland (German musicologist), 18–19n10, 21n2
Schumann, Clara née Wieck (1819–1896, German pianist, composer, and wife of Robert Schumann), 153–54, 161, 161–62n16, 166, 167–68, 175
Schumann, Robert (1810–1856, German composer and music critic), 153, 154–56, 158–61, 162, 165, 165n22, 169, 172, 174, 175, 209
  Overture, Scherzo and Finale, op. 52, 163

INDEX

Schröder-Devrient, Wilhelmine (1804–1860, German operatic soprano), 155, 156–58
Scott, Sir Walter (1771–1832, Scottish novelist), 59
Scribe, Augustin-Eugène (1791–1861, French dramatist and librettist), 48, 50, 51, 55, 58, 70, 71, 76, 79, 80, 82, 89, 134
Semper, Gottfried (1803–1879, German architect), 180
Shakespeare, William (1564–1616, English playwright and poet), 98, 205
Shaw, George Bernard (1856–1950, Irish playwright and music critic under pen name Corno di Bassetto), 98–99, 210
Spohr, Louis (1784–1859, German composer), 160
Spontini, Gaspare (1774–1851, Italian composer)
  La Vestale, 210
Sposato, Jeffrey S. (American musicologist), 164
Staatsbibliothek zu Berlin, 18–19n10, 21n2
Starr, Mark (American musicologist), 24
Stern, Julius (1820–1883, German conductor), 134
Stolz, Rosine (1815–1903, French operatic mezzo-soprano), 70–71
Storrs, Ronald (1881–1955, military governor of Jerusalem), 190n11

Sullivan, Arthur (1842–1900, English composer), 57

T

Tchaikovsky, Pyotr (1840–1893, Russian composer), 313
Teatro alla Scala, Milan, 35–37, 189
Teatro La Fenice, Venice, 39, 43
Teatro Nuovo, Padua, 30
Teatro Regio, Turin, 31
Teatro San Benedetto, Venice, 33
Theater an der Wien, Vienna, 73
Théâtre Impérial de l'Opéra Comique, Paris, 48–50
Théâtre Royal Italien, Paris, 43, 45, 48
Théâtre Royal de l'Odéon, Paris, 45–48
Thomas, Ambroise (1811–1896, French composer)
  Hamlet, 142
  Mignon, 142
Thornton, Elaine (English writer), 14n7
Titus (real name Flavius Vespasianus, emperor of Rome, 79–81 CE), 15
Toscanini, Arturo (1867–1957, Italian conductor), 197–98, 197n17
Tosta, Volker (German musicologist), 27

V

Velluti, Giovanni Battista (1780–1861, Italian operatic castrato), 40–41

Verdi, Giuseppe (1813–1901, Italian composer), 95n7, 142, 208, 210
  Un ballo in maschera, 87
  Don Carlos, 137
  Ernani, 79
  Rigoletto, 141, 192
  La Traviata, 53, 141, 142, 192, 213
  Il Trovatore, 84, 141, 144
  Les Vêpres Siciliennes, 137
Verne, Jules (1828–1905, French novelist), 66–67
Véron, Louis-Désiré (1798–1867, manager Paris Opéra 1831–1835), 51
Viardot-Garcia, Pauline (1821–1910, French operatic mezzo-soprano and composer), 74
Vivaldi, Antonio (1678–1741, Italian composer), 1–2, 5, 9
  Le quattro stagioni, 1
Vogler, Georg Joseph (1749–1814, German composer and pedagogue), 20–21, 23, 25
  "Master's fugue," 19

W

Wagner, Cosima. *See* Bülow, Cosima von
Wagner, Gottfried (German musicologist, great-grandson of RW), 170n9
Wagner, Minna née Planer (d. 1866, first wife of Richard Wagner), 181
Wagner, Richard (1813–1883, German composer), 5–6, 54, 61, 68–69, 87, 122–23, 138, 139–40, 141, 146–47, 165, 166–82, 181–82n15, 183, 186, 197–98n17, 198, 199, 200, 201, 202, 204–5, 206–8, 210, 212
  Der Fliegende Holländer, 123, 142, 180
  Götterdämmerung, 142, 146
  Das Judenthum in der Musik, 5–6, 7–8, 170–80
  Lohengrin, 142, 197
  Die Meistersinger von Nürnberg, 168, 172, 213
  Parsifal, 54, 142, 146, 180, 181
  Das Rheingold, 142
  Rienzi, 123
  Der Ring des Nibelungen, 172
  Siegfried, 213
  Tannhäuser, 213
  Tristan und Isolda, 145
Walker, Alan (English-Canadian musicologist), 161, 161–62n16
Weber, Bernhard Anselm (1764–1821, German composer), 19
Weber, Carl Maria von (1786–1826, German composer), 21, 22, 27, 34, 39, 126–28
  Abu Hasan, 25, 27
  Les Bohémiens, 48
  Die drei Pintos, 127–30
  Der Freischütz, 68, 210
Weber, Caroline née Brandt (1794–1852, wife of Carl Maria von Weber), 126–29

Weber, Max von (1822–1881, son of Carl Maria von Weber and Caroline), 129
Weininger, Otto (1880–1903, German philosopher), 180
Weitsch, Friedrich Georg (1758–1828, German artist), 17
Whitman, Walt (1819–1892, American poet), 78–79
Winkler, Hofrat Karl Gottlieb Theodor (1775–1856, vice-director of Dresden theaters), 128
Wolfssohn, Aaron (1754–1835, German-Jewish Bible critic), 17, 20, 24
Wulff, Ester née Bamberger (1740–1822, maternal grandmother of Meyerbeer), 13n4
Wulff, Hanka (1770–1847, aunt of Meyerbeer), 13n4
Wulff, Jette (1779–1852, aunt of Meyerbeer), 13n4
Wulff, Liepmann Meyer (1745–1812, maternal grandfather, early patron of Meyerbeer), 13, 22
Wulff, Malka. *See* Beer, Amalia
Wulff, Sara (1774–1832, aunt of Meyerbeer), 13n4

Z

Zak, Jonathan (Israeli pianist), 199–200
Zion Hall, Jerusalem, 195

ST. CLAIR SHORES PUBLIC LIBRARY
22500 ELEVEN MILE ROAD
ST. CLAIR SHORES, MI 48081